STREET WISE

A Programme for Educating Young People about Citizenship, Rights, Responsibilities and the Law

SAM FRANKEL

Foreword by Bishop Tim Stevens

Jessica Kingsley Publishers
London and Philadelphia

Please note that this material has been produced for educational purposes only, to promote awareness and understanding of the issues. If a question of law arises as a result of the course individuals should seek legal advice – information on doing this has been included within the sessions.

The content of this book is based on the law, as of the time of writing, in England and Wales. Many of the principles and ideas apply equally in other jurisdictions, although there are variations, both in terms of what actions are defined as crimes and how the law is applied out on the streets. For more information on regional differences, facilitators are encouraged to follow up web links included in the sessions.

First published in 2009
by Jessica Kingsley Publishers
116 Pentonville Road
London N1 9JB, UK
and
400 Market Street, Suite 400
Philadelphia, PA 19106, USA

www.jkp.com

Library of Congress Cataloging-in-Publication Data

Frankel, Sam.
 Street wise : a programme for educating young people about citizenship, rights, responsibilities and the law / Sam Frankel, Tim Stevens, and Al Aynsley-Green ; foreword Tim Stevens.
  p. cm.
 Includes bibliographical references and index.
  ISBN 978-1-84310-680-7 (pb : alk. paper) 1. Youth--Life skills guides--Study and teaching. 2. Youth--Conduct of life--Study and teaching. I. Aynsley-Green, A. II. Stevens, Tim, 1967- III. Title.
 HQ796.F762 2009
 646.700835--dc22

                                          2008035537

British Library Cataloguing in Publication Data
A CIP catalogue record for this book is available from the British Library

ISBN 978 1 84310 680 7

Printed and bound in Great Britain by
Athenaeum Press, Gateshead, Tyne and Wear

STREET WISE

CONTENTS

List of exercises

List of handouts

Session 5

ACKNOWLEDGEMENTS

I would like to thank the following people: Tom McDonnell for his guidance on Scottish law; also Kate Egerton, Gavin Dingwall and particularly Ali Roberts for their thoughts and advice on the material; all the young people who have helped shape the material over a number of years; those at Act 4 who have supported me in writing this book; and especially Raman Bedi and Terry and Gill Over for their ongoing encouragement, friendship and help.

My special thanks to Allison James for giving me the confidence to express my thoughts, and to Peter Lloyd, who was involved in the original conception of some of the material and whose friendship, expertise and wisdom encouraged me to take the ideas further.

I am enormously grateful to those who have given me the time and space to write: to both sets of parents, to my children Ruari and Rosie, and to my wife, Moira – thank you!

FOREWORD

This book is an important contribution to the prominent discourse around young people out on the streets. However, rather than simply seeing young people as a problem, the material within this book seeks to equip young people with the knowledge and skills needed to be seen as a constructive force within their communities.

As a course the material is creative, informative and relevant, providing facilitators with an easy to use resource, which can engage young people with the issues. Through themes such as stereotypes, right and wrong and the criminal law, young people will understand better both their rights and responsibilities out on the streets, recognising how they fit into society as a whole.

By seeking to encourage greater mutual respect between young people and adults this book provides an important foundation on which young people can build as they take greater responsibility as active citizens within their communities.

The Right Reverend Tim Stevens, Bishop of Leicester,
Chair of The Children's Society

STREET WISE: A PROGRAMME

INTRODUCTION

This material has been written for teachers, youth workers, social workers and many others who work with young people. It is aimed at providing relevant and creative ideas and information to support you, as key adults, in the work that you do. The material has been designed to be flexible so that it can be used in a variety of settings, ways and with different types of groups. Fundamentally, it offers an opportunity to engage with some important issues that impact on young people's everyday lives, strengthening their understanding and practical ability to demonstrate their part as a constructive force within their communities.

Point and purpose

Young people's actions, particularly out on the streets, face unprecedented scrutiny. Fears of gun and knife crime, alcohol abuse, vandalism and damage, antisocial behaviour, to name but a few, have led legislators, on behalf of communities, to increase laws and thereby their ability to control, supervise and ultimately punish young people. However, the point and purpose of this course is that only by inviting young people to become partners in their communities can these issues start to be addressed. The course therefore seeks to equip young people with the knowledge and skills they need to understand their rights and responsibilities, so that they can put them into practice by actively assuming their role as citizens, allowing them and those around them to make the most of the communities that they share.

Ethos

The material contained in the sessions seeks to provide a well-informed, interactive and relevant method of investigating the issues. The material is designed to encourage learning by inviting the participants to get involved. It is therefore important that an environment is created within which they feel that they can do this. (Note later comments about ground rules.) As a result of this process groups will grow together as a team, maximising what they take from the sessions in terms of both knowledge and enjoyment.

SUMMARY OF SESSIONS

Session 1: Young people and society

This session invites young people to think about how they fit into their community. By looking at stereotypes of young people it becomes clear that these are not always positive, with some adults seeing young people as a threat. This gets in the way of young people having the freedom and respect within society that they deserve. This session will invite participants to think about how to challenge these stereotypes and get involved in changing attitudes and opinions. It will introduce listening skills, exploring how they can be used to help show respect and receive it.

Session 2: Right and wrong

This session will ask participants to think about their actions and how they impact on the way in which they are seen. It will ask how we know what actions are right and wrong – who defines this? Knowing what is and is not acceptable is not always straightforward. However, reflecting on 'feelings' can make it easier to attach meaning to our actions. Participants will be encouraged to spend a bit of time thinking about different situations from the point of view of others, including looking at victims of crime. By the end of the session the participants will recognise the important principle that we all have a right to feel safe and a responsibility to make sure others feel safe too.

Session 3: It's a crime

Knowing what is right and wrong is one thing, standing up for it is another. The session starts by asking young people to think about peer pressure, looking at constructive ways in which we can share our thoughts and feelings. The session goes on to look at the purpose of the criminal law, before focusing in on the type of behaviours that it deals with. The session ends by considering the impact that breaking the law can have on offenders, as well as challenging the participants to recognise that the role of enforcing the law is for everyone.

Session 4: Street law

In being a citizen it is important that, as well as realising individual responsibilities, we are also aware of our rights. This session will look at some of the powers the police have and how they can be used. It will look particularly at issues around stop and search, arrest, and what happens after an arrest when someone arrives at the police station. If young people come into contact with the police, the information in this session will help them to understand better what the police can do as part of their job, but also what they have to do, in order to respect the rights of citizens.

Session 5: Citizenship in practice

This session will remind participants about how important respect is in breaking down barriers and in building effective relationships, and will review other specific themes from previous sessions. By following a case study, participants will have to use the knowledge and skills they have picked up during the course to complete the tasks, in a sequence that takes them from speaking with a victim to experiencing a police interview.

GETTING A COURSE STARTED
Your role

The role of the facilitator is to guide the group through the sessions. You do not need to be an expert in the themes covered in the course, as all you need has been provided. There will, however, be an element of preparation, and a reliance on your knowledge of those you are working with, in adapting the material so that it is fully effective for them. It is helpful if the role of facilitator can be shared with another. This allows you to split the workload, as well as providing another voice to reinforce the information shared, and support with group management (particularly valuable if some members of the group have a tendency to be disruptive).

Your participants

The material is aimed at young people aged around 15 years and above (although there is scope for the material to be adapted for groups below this age). There is no need to have worked with the participants before. Similarly, the nature of the material means that it is just as relevant to young people who have been in trouble with the police as it is to those that have not.

Running a course

The way in which you run the course will depend on the context within which you are working, but the material has been set out in five 90-minute sessions, to be used with a group of up to 20 young people. (Note the later section on adaptability for alternative ways to use the material, including specifically within the school timetable.) Do make sure that the space within which you run the sessions is appropriate and that there is sufficient room for groupwork. You will need a good supply of pens and paper and access to a flipchart or whiteboard.

Facilitating a session

- **Overview**: Provides you with an introduction to each session. It outlines the themes to be discussed and highlights some specific pointers to guide you through that session.

- **Aims and outcomes**: Each session offers a clear set of aims and expected outcomes. However, by engaging with some of the additional themes covered in the 'Notes', you will be able to extend these.

- **Timed outline**: A structure has been provided for each session. To follow the core course, which deals with the main points from each session, use the 'Timed outlines' and follow the sections in this font (see point 2, p.27), either reading or paraphrasing the text within them. The outlines act as an *aide-mémoire*, not only in relation to content but also highlighting handouts and suggested timings for each section. There is also space to make your own notes.

- **Introduction to session**: This is your opportunity to deal with any 'housekeeping' considerations, as well as address more formally issues such as the ethos of the course, ground rules and, of course, the structure of the session itself. You will find it useful to have a flipchart, or equivalent, to use for writing up information such as ground rules and the running order for each session.

  - *Ground rules*: The nature of the material means that it is important to ensure that certain ground rules are in place before the sessions start. Even if you are using this material in school, it would still be useful to discuss ground rules, establishing a basis on which to engage with the issues and how to work together. It is important that the ground rules are drawn up and agreed by the group as a whole. Focus in on rules that allow positive communication – for example, not interrupting, accepting each other's opinions. Also include more general rules, such as what should happen with mobile phones during the sessions, and that you will end sessions on time. Confidentiality is obviously very important. Do make sure that any ground rules in relation to confidentiality are linked in to child protection policies, making clear any responsibility you might have to report information shared, if it causes you particular concern.

  - *Icebreakers*: The need for 'icebreakers' will be dependent on the group. However, if the group is not bonding, or is finding it difficult to share thoughts and feelings, do consider using an icebreaker. An icebreaker does not need to be complicated, and can be as simple as asking the group to share their names and something about themselves. Alternatively, it might involve moving around, finding someone else with a birthday in the same month, or lining themselves up in alphabetical order. However, ultimately the type of icebreaker you use depends on the group. Examples of additional icebreaker activities are provided in the following.

    - For groups who do not know each other: ask them to try and discover something in common (outside of school or youth group) with as many other people in the group as possible. Once everyone is sitting again, the challenge is to see if they can remember what these are.

    - A more general activity involves everyone writing something funny that has happened to them on a piece of paper, which is then passed to the facilitator. The facilitator reads them out and the group has to guess who each might refer to.

○ For paired groups: get one person to draw a picture. They then have to describe the picture to the other person who then attempts to see how close they can get to drawing an exact replica.

- **Exercises**: There are two types of exercise: 'shared exercises', involving everyone in the session, or 'group exercises', in which participants should be split into groups of, ideally, no more than five. Other exercises that need a slightly different approach, or where there is a more obvious choice, will be indicated. Each exercise is explained by following the 'Instructions' and the 'Questions'. The exercises are brought together by a 'Discuss' section, which highlights the key themes that are worth reflecting on following the practical aspect of the exercise. Handouts will be needed for certain exercises, and these can simply be photocopied and used. Guidance on which handouts and related documents are required can be found in the 'Timed outlines' as well as in the 'Instructions' for the exercise. Note that some resources for the exercises will need to be prepared prior to the session.

- **Notes**: Throughout each chapter 'Notes' have been included to provide facilitators with additional background information related to the themes. These can be used simply to provide you with further knowledge to share if relevant during discussions, or can be used more actively, within the sessions, as discussion starters or as material for reflection at other times – for example, as part of further investigation into the themes. You may wish to simply copy some of these notes for participants to look at in their own time.

- **Conclusion**: This is an opportunity for facilitators to draw together the themes of the session. It is a further chance to deal with any housekeeping matters, such as when the next session is. You may also find that it becomes a time to check participants' well-being, for example that they have not been negatively affected by dealing with some of the themes. It will be important for you to make note of any support agencies – those suggested in the book, or others known to you, towards which you may wish to guide participants, as necessary.

- **Project ideas**: At the end of each of Sessions 1–4 are some practical ideas for projects that you may wish to develop with your group. They provide suggestions on how young people can get more involved in taking on their role as active citizens, and taking a lead in making the most of their communities.

- **Helpful websites**: Relevant websites for each session are listed at the end of Sessions 1–4. These include sites that facilitators or participants may wish to look at for further information, advice or help.

- **Bibliography: References and further reading**: Any references referred to in the session are listed at the end. This section also includes other material that may be worth looking at.

ADAPTABILITY

Notwithstanding the way in which this material has been laid out, there is scope for it to be used in different contexts, for example on a one-to-one basis or in a classroom. Use your knowledge and experience to work with the materials, adapting them as you see fit so that they are effective for those with whom you work – for example, bringing in additional support facilitators to help with reading difficulties or focusing in on those issues that you know have particular resonance with your group.

In school

The course has obvious application within the Citizenship Curriculum for both Key Stages 3 and 4, addressing topics that form part of the 'knowledge and understanding about becoming informed citizens', as well as supporting young people to develop not only their 'skills of enquiry and communication', but also their 'skills of participation and responsible action'. Elements of the course can also be used in other areas of the curriculum, for example within Key Stage 4 Religious Studies, providing discussions and practical examples within the context of applied ethics. Obviously, you could also run your own 'Street Wise Course' as an extra-curricular activity. This might be something that parents, as well as young people, are interested in attending.

Timings: Within schools it may be hard to identify an hour-and-a-half to run a session, or you may just wish to look at a particular issue within a lesson. The sessions themselves can be split in half, effectively creating ten 50–60-minute sessions that could be used within the timetable. By splitting the sessions to fit within a lesson, you will also find that there is slightly more time to engage with some of the issues raised in the 'Notes' sections and to look at the 'Project ideas'. However, do be aware that, in order to create continuity between the sessions and/or the context for a particular exercise, you will need to have a good understanding of the material as a whole.

Differentiation: There is plenty of scope within the exercises for them to be adapted to participants of different abilities. For example, there are a number of exercises that rely on the participants reading material, which can be dealt with by turning the task into an oral exercise, or by having additional help from other participants or adults.

SUMMARY

Many of the themes in this book maintain a high profile within society today. It is so important that young people are encouraged to engage with these issues, and it is hoped that the material in this book will allow you to do just that. Young people need to be aware that, in discourses around citizenship and crime, they are not simply the problem, but rather they are part of the solution. It is only by equipping young people to see themselves in this way that we as a society can effectively move forward and improve our communities for the better.

NOTES RELATING TO USE IN SCOTLAND

There are some significant differences with the law as it applies in England, Wales and Northern Ireland from that in Scotland. The notes below highlight some of these differences, which you will need to be aware of as you work through the sessions, although the general principles remain the same. For more information please note the specific links below.

Session 3 – Sheets 3.5a and 3.5b

This exercise looks at aspects of the criminal law in detail. In Scotland, the answers do remain the same, except for question 3a. However, there are variations in the legislation that these offences fall under. Differences you may wish to be aware of for this exercise are noted below. In Scottish law:

1a) Anya and Ben are aged 17 years old and Charlie 14 years (clarification to question)

2. there is no GBH, rather 'assault to severe injury'

3a) answer is yes, as age of criminal responsibility is 8 years

3b) burglary would be dealt with as housebreaking

3c) handling would be dealt with as reset

4. various legislation might be used in this scenario, including that which applies to malicious mischief or vandalism

5a) this offence would probably be dealt with as breach of the peace.

Sessions 4 and 5

Both these sessions look at the application of the criminal process to young people out on the streets. The variations for young people in Scotland as distinct from elsewhere in the UK are outlined below, and this information can be used to help you adapt the materials accordingly.

STOP AND SEARCH

The principles of stop and search in Scotland are the same as in England and Wales, although the powers of the police in Scotland emanate from different legal sources to the law in England and Wales, and the same test of reasonable suspicion applies. Individuals also have the right to know:

• why they have been stopped

• that they cannot be asked to remove more than outer clothing out on the streets

• that they can have a record of the search, which they can get from the police station.

Police powers to search are more extensive in Scotland than in England and Wales, as the person is seen to be 'detained' (see notes on arrest below).

Scotland does not have Police Community Support Officers (PCSOs), preferring for such duties to remain under the responsibility of police constables. There is a community warden scheme that is concerned with antisocial behaviour, but without the powers of the PCSOs in England and Wales.

ARREST AND DETENTION

In England and Wales police can arrest on suspicion of an offence. In Scotland police do not use arrest until they feel there is sufficient evidence for the case to be put in front of the courts, to start criminal proceedings. Out on the streets, therefore, individuals can be 'detained' prior to arrest.

Where a police officer has reasonable grounds for suspecting that an offence has been, or is being, committed for which the punishment, if guilty, is prison, then, in order to investigate the offence, an individual can be required to go with the officer to a police station or other places thought to help with the investigation.

Detention can also be used to require individuals to remain with the police out on the streets, while their name and addresses are checked or they give an explanation in response to the officer's suspicion of their connection with an offence. Witnesses can also be detained and asked to provide their name and address. If they refuse, this is an offence.

On detention an officer must inform the person detained:

- of his or her suspicion and the general nature of the offence which the person is suspected to have committed

- why they are being detained (this might be for a search, to explain what they saw if they were a witness, or to be taken to a police station for questioning), and that they must remain with the officer, otherwise they will be committing an offence

- that they do not have to answer questions other than to give their name and address, date of birth, place of birth and nationality.

ARRIVING AT THE POLICE STATION

The detained person must be taken to the police station (or other places relating to the investigation) as soon as possible. On arrival they have the right to:

- have a person they name to be informed of their detention or arrest (note this call will be made by the police; the detained person does not have the right to speak in person)

- have a solicitor informed of their detention or arrest.

Information similar to that on the custody record in England and Wales must be kept in Scotland, such as the place where detention started, the place to which the detained person was taken, nature of the suspected offence, time detention started and when the detained person was informed of their rights, and their response to this.

If detained a person can only be held for six hours from the time of their detention. Once released, they cannot be detained on the same grounds again.

UNDER 16S

If the individual is under 16 years, then the police must make contact with their parents or those that have custody of that person as soon as possible on their arrival at the police station. The police, on arrest, will also look into releasing that person from the police station to their parents as soon as possible, or holding them somewhere other than a police station, unless this is not practical or the offence is very serious.

POLICE INTERVIEWS

Police interviews throughout the UK must be conducted in a way that is fair, if it is to be admitted as evidence in court. The principle of the exercise in Session 5 remains the same, although in practice some details might be slightly different.

Session 1

YOUNG PEOPLE AND SOCIETY

SESSION OVERVIEW

Session 1 invites young people to think about how they are seen and how they want to be seen within their communities. Before going on to look at rights and responsibilities and the role of the criminal law in later sessions, it is important that young people recognise the context within which they live. Unfortunately, that context is not as positive and supportive as it could be. By looking at some of the stereotypes that adults apply to young people, we see how young people are often portrayed as posing a threat to their communities. Even though this perspective is a long way from reality in the case of the majority of young people, it still serves to colour the relationship between the two groups. This session invites young people to consider the implications of such barriers, and how these barriers can be broken down. It invites the participants to explore the notion of respect and the role this can play in promoting relationships. However, respect is only effective as a two-way process and the session ends by introducing some practical communication techniques that young people can use to take the lead in building relationships and fostering an attitude of respect with those around them.

Aims

- to explore how young people perceive themselves and are perceived by others
- to consider the power of stereotypes
- to explore some of the negative views associated with young people out in society
- to consider the importance of breaking down barriers
- to investigate practically the effectiveness of listening skills in building relationships.

Session 1 timed outline

ACTION	TIME IN MINUTES	DESCRIPTION	RESOURCES	NOTES
1. Introduction	10	• welcome to the course • outline ethos (to empower young people as citizens within their communities) • explain how the sessions will run • go through ground rules and introductions	Flipchart Badges	
2. Society and you	10	Put descriptive words around room, or on table, and ask participants to choose: • What words best describe YOU while you are out in the neighbourhood? • What words describe how you think adults see YOU while you are out in the neighbourhood? Discuss contrasting responses to above questions.	1.2a 1.2b 1.2c	
3. Stereotypes	10	Stereotypes are a way of ordering the social world. • What stereotypes do you use? • What are the dangers of using stereotypes? The danger of seeing the world through stereotypes: • lack accuracy • are seen as applying universally • damage relationships • impact on policy and practice • desire to fulfil stereotypes leads to difference.		
4. Young people as a threat	10	Stereotypes have been associated with young people for many thousands of years. • historical quotes round the room – participants to put them in date order • what is the common theme from these quotes? The common theme is that young people are seen by adults as a threat to social harmony that needs to be controlled. This threat, reflected in the media, also impacts on what becomes policy. Important that stereotypes of young people as a threat should be considered alongside facts that reflect reality.	1.4	

Session 1 timed outline *continued*

ACTION	TIME IN MINUTES	DESCRIPTION	RESOURCES	NOTES
5. Break	5			
6. Breaking down barriers	15	Seeing young people as a threat acts as a barrier to relationships and limits their interest in taking on their role as citizens. ● share scenario and questions Unfair stereotypes can lead to individuals withdrawing themselves from society and not engaging fully with it. However, young people do have a responsibility to demonstrate that these stereotypes are wrong.		
7. What is respect?	25	Communities would be easier places to live if those within it…each other. Mutual respect is not complicated. It is about trying to understand issues from the perspectives of others. ● quiz ● how do you feel when respected/not respected? ● how do you show respect?		
8. Showing respect		One way of showing respect is by listening to what others say. Listening exercise: in three parts. 1. road blocks to listening 2. nonverbal communication 3. open questions.		
9. Conclusion		1. review session 2. feedback from session 3. details of next session. NB Before the next session participants may be encouraged to: ● use listening skills ● take on one of the 'Project ideas'.		

Outcomes

Session outcomes will include participants:

- working together as a team

- thinking more about how they are seen when out in their communities

- being able to recognise stereotypes and their dangers

- recognising specific stereotypes held in relation to young people

- realising that they have a role to play in breaking down barriers and overturning stereotypes

- understanding what is meant by mutual respect

- using listening skills as a means of showing respect.

Outcomes

1.1 INTRODUCTION TO SESSION 1

Welcome

1. **Welcome the group and perform introductions**

   This first session is important, as it sets the tone for the programme as a whole. As discussed in the previous chapter, this may not be the first time that you have worked with this group, but even so, it is helpful for the participants to realise that they are about to embark with you on a new programme of learning, where their involvement will make all the difference. This is a good opportunity for you and the participants to introduce yourselves; you may wish to do this in a creative way (see notes on icebreakers on p.16). Use name badges if helpful.

2. **Provide a brief outline of the programme**

   Young people out in the neighbourhood are often a target for adults who see them as a nuisance and as a threat, with the result that young people are not treated with the respect they deserve. This course is designed to help *you* change this. It will ask you to think about how you want to be seen by others, what behaviour is right and what is wrong, why the law covers certain behaviour and what the law says and can do. It will help you to recognise that you have certain rights, but also that these rights are only really effective when you recognise your responsibilities as well. By the end of the programme you should be better equipped to know your rights and responsibilities within your community – and take on your role as an active citizen.

3. **Ethos of programme**

   Each session will ask you to get involved in thinking about different themes relevant to your everyday lives. It will also ask you to put into practice new skills that can help you in your relationships with others. You will be able to make the most of these sessions if you think openly about the topics, discuss them honestly and enjoy them.

4. **Ground rules**

   See p.16. Even if you have worked with this group before, considering ground rules will help with creating freedom and safety to engage with the topics.

Introduce Session 1

This session gives you the chance to think about how you fit into your community. You will need to think about how you see yourself and the way in which others see young people. Stereotypes of young people are not always positive, some adults see young people as a threat. This gets in the way of young people having the freedom and respect within society that they deserve. This session will invite you to think about how you can challenge those stereotypes and get involved in changing attitudes and opinions. It will introduce skills you can try to use to help you show respect and receive it. The outline of this session is as follows:

1. Introduction to Session 1
2. Society and you
3. Stereotypes
4. Young people as a threat
5. Break
6. Breaking down barriers
7. What is respect?
8. Showing respect
9. Conclusion to Session 1.

1.2 SOCIETY AND YOU

Shared exercise 1.2: The way you are seen

Instructions: Use the descriptive words on Sheet 1.2a, adding any others that you think might be appropriate (or leaving space for the participants to add their own). Copy the words and cut them out, making sure there are enough words for each participant to choose a couple in answering the questions. In response to Questions 1 and 2 below, participants will need to pick one of the words, which they can then place on the appropriate figure (Sheets 1.2b and 1.2c – these can be enlarged or simply copied onto flipchart paper). Getting participants to sign the words they choose could help to focus discussion. You can ask the questions at the same time, or one after the other.

Question 1: What words best describe YOU while you are out in the neighbourhood?

Question 2: What words describe how you think adults see YOU while you are out in the neighbourhood?

Discuss: Contrast the answers to Question 2 with those to Question 1, exploring whether there is any difference – and if there is, why that might be.

As will emerge as the chapter continues, there is often a contrast between the way young people regard their behaviour when out on the streets, and the way it is seen by adults. The session goes on to explore the nature of that adult perception and how it can be linked more closely to reality. However, if members of your group find that their view of themselves matches a negative adult view, then the session will challenge them to consider whether such behaviour is the best way to make the most of the community that they live in.

THE WAY YOU ARE SEEN (1)

Helpful	Rude	Protecting	Have fun
Aggressive	A danger	Frightening	Noisy
Look out for others	Spend time with friends	Don't bother others	Always bother others
Mind my own business			

THE WAY YOU ARE SEEN (2)

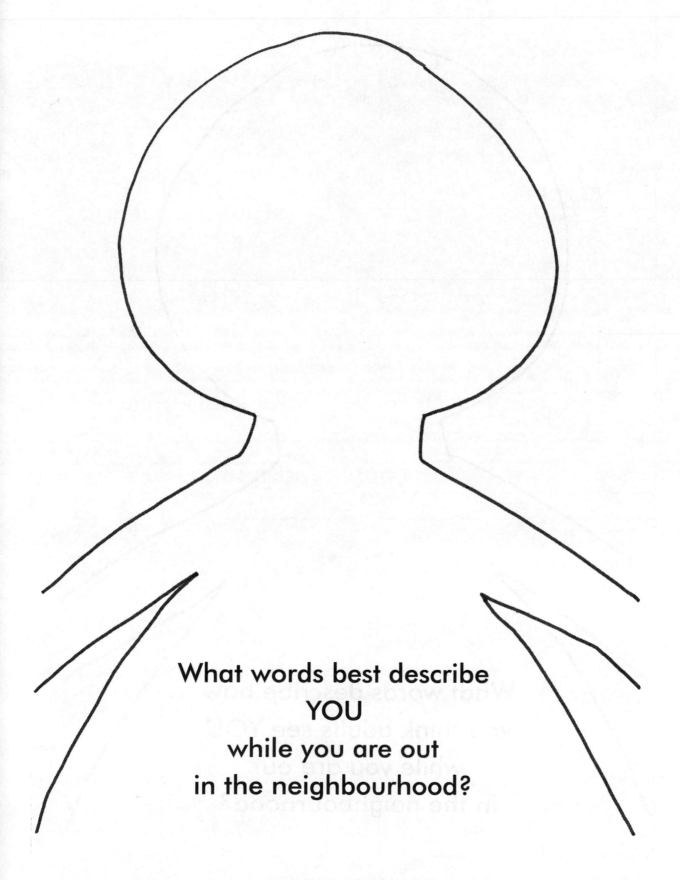

What words best describe
YOU
while you are out
in the neighbourhood?

THE WAY YOU ARE SEEN (3)

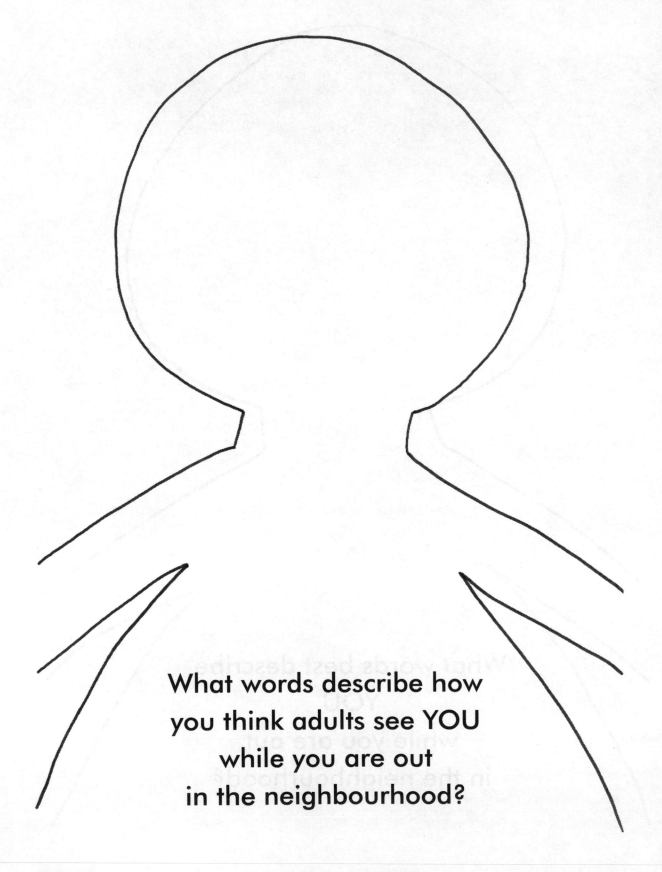

What words describe how
you think adults see YOU
while you are out
in the neighbourhood?

1.3 STEREOTYPES

What are stereotypes?

Stereotypes provide us all with a quick and easy way of making sense of the world around us. By using stereotypes we look to put people into different categories and from this attach meaning, to guide us in how we react to them. In order to do this we take into account factors such as clothing, gender, age, ethnicity, speech, body shape, and what others can and cannot do. Stereotypes are an important element to understand about the way in which adults and young people view each other and how they interact.

Shared exercise 1.3: Stereotypes

Question 1: What stereotypes do you use/are you aware of?

Question 2: What are the dangers of using stereotypes?

The danger of stereotypes

Stereotypes:

- lack accuracy

- are applied too broadly – individual characteristics are overlooked

- distort our view of groups, and consequently damage relationships

- can impact negatively on policy and practice

- can lead groups to exaggerate their differences in their desire to fulfil stereotypes, building up barriers to others.

NOTES

Accuracy and interpretation: One danger of stereotypes is that they take on universal meaning, being applied to everyone within a particular 'group'. When this is done with a lack of accuracy, these stereotypes become very harmful, impacting not only on the way those who are seen to fall within that group are spoken about, but also on how they are treated. Stereotypes can become the accepted way of thinking about those within a group, with no recognition of different individual characteristics. If misunderstanding which results from stereotyping is not challenged, then it can result in relationships between social groups being severely damaged. (A particularly telling example of this is the race riots of the early 1980s.)

Exaggerate difference: Stereotypes are also a consequence of our desire to be seen to belong. This need to belong is particularly acute during teenage years, as young people become increasingly conscious of how they define themselves in the context of those around them, particularly their peer group. Stereotypes become a means by which groups can identify others with whom they have similarities, and so are happy to associate with, in contrast to those who are different, and therefore avoided or targeted. Being able to identify difference quickly and visibly makes it easier to assert your own bond, or sense of belonging, with 'your' group. One example of this is clothing styles within youth culture, such as the difference between 'townies' and 'goths'.

1.4 YOUNG PEOPLE AS A THREAT

Stereotypes have been associated with young people throughout history. This exercise invites you to think about a stereotype that has had a negative effect on young people.

Exercise 1.4: Match the date to the quote

Instructions: Having copied Sheet 1.4, ask the participants individually, in pairs or in groups to match the date to the quote. This can be done simply sitting together in the group, or the quotes can be displayed around the room and the participants invited each to stick what they think is the right date against quotes, writing their initials on their stickers.

DO EXERCISE.

Answers

- *Quote 1*: 1961 AD – a report from the British Medical Association (Pearson 1983: 17).

- *Quote 2*: 480s BC – the words of the philosopher Socrates (Brake 1980: 1).

- *Quote 3*: 1600s AD – based on the words from *A Winter's Tale* by William Shakespeare (Shakespeare 1905: 337).

- *Quote 4*: 800s BC – the words of Greek poet Hesiod (Cote 1994: xi).

Question: What is the common theme from these quotes? (The following section invites you to explore further the theme of young people as a threat that runs through the quotes.)

Young people have for thousands of years been seen as a threat to society. They are seen as a destructive presence at risk of damaging what adults see as the proper way of life. This view of young people still exists today and it remains a recurring theme within the media. These are examples of terms recently used in the press in relation to young people:

- 'yobs' – *The Sun* (16/6/08)

- 'feral gangs' – *Daily Express* (27/2/08)

- 'juveniles' – *Daily Mail* (16/6/08)

- 'tearaways' – *The Telegraph* (18/3/08)

- 'thugs' – *Daily Mirror* (27/5/08)

- 'psychotic oiks' – *The Sunday Times* (20/1/08).

'MATCH THE DATE TO THE QUOTE' EXERCISE

1961 AD

800s BC

480s BC

1600s AD

Which date fits with which quote?

1) Looked at in his worst light the adolescent can take on an alarming aspect: he has learned no definite moral standards from his parents, is contemptuous of the law, easily bored…

2) The young of today love luxury. They have bad manners, they scoff at authority and lack respect for their elders. Children nowadays are real tyrants, they no longer stand up when their elders come into a room where they are sitting, they contradict their parents, chat together in the presence of adults, eat gluttonously and tyrannise their teachers.

3) I wish there was no age between sixteen and twenty three, or if there were, people would sleep through it, because what happens during this time is men getting women with child, upsetting old people, stealing and fighting.

4) There is no future for society if it is to depend on the frivolous youth of today, for certainly all youths are reckless beyond words.

NOTES: MORAL PANICS

Stereotypes in the media: Terms such as those just displayed provide a means by which the stereotypes are reinforced. Indeed, analysis of the newspapers show that there are more negative stories about young people in the press than positive, and that the majority of these reports relate to young people's involvement in antisocial or criminal behaviour. [1]The active role of the media in reinforcing these views is highlighted in *The Sun*'s newspaper campaign 'shop a yob' (www.thesun.co.uk), where members of the public can report young people behaving badly. Notably, the media do not so obviously promote opportunities to single out young people acting positively within their communities.

Panic and power: The consequences of the continuation of such stereotypes are 'moral panics'. The term was developed by academic Stanley Cohen in 1972, as a tool for reflecting on over-reaction to the perceived behaviour of a particular social group. Cohen argues that in order to have a moral panic you need: (1) a suitable enemy; (2) a suitable victim; and (3) the belief that the problem will pervade all of society unless something is done (Cohen 2002). Once these elements are created, the stereotypes develop as 'accepted truth', shaping and guiding both policy and practice. The power to create these elements, to identify the enemy, victim and problem, often lies in the hands of the powerful, such as those with access to a publicity machine – which in turn highlights a larger moral issue around the way in which such panics are used to engineer public opinion and the law, in order for the powerful to protect themselves (an argument you may wish to revisit in Session 3). Nowhere is this argument more defined than in relation to young people and successive governments since the mid-1990s.

Controlling young people: A build-up of press interest in young people during the late 1980s was brought to a climax with the murder of James Bulger in 1993. The killing of a boy a month away from his third birthday by two ten-year-olds resulted in a panic that was so intense that it was seen by some to go beyond a moral panic and become a total panic (Brown 1998). Public reaction, encouraged by the media, saw politicians quickly call into being punitive laws that would ensure the threat presented by young people was firmly controlled and any perpetrators constrained. New Labour, in the run-up to, and on reaching, power, took even further this harsh approach to young people (Bell 1999). Since then successive criminal legislation has focused on the need to demonstrate a firm and punitive approach to dealing with youth crime, exemplified by the fact that the number of young people being sent to prison has doubled since James Bulger's death (Muncie 2004).

The truth: This desire to combat the perceived threat posed by young people as frequent offenders damaging the harmony of community life must be seen in the context of reality.

- Adults commit more than 75 per cent of all detected crime (Muncie 2004). See www.youthinformation.com.

---

[1]   This was first shown by Porteous and Colston (1980) and reinforced more recently by the charity Children's Express (Neustatter 1998). This theme continues to remain an issue for young people themselves as shown in current work by Headliners (formerly Children's Express), www.headliners.org.

- Children aged under one year are more at risk of murder than any other age group, with parents being the most likely perpetrators (Muncie 2004).

- Young people are far more likely to be the victims of crime than the perpetrators – a recent report showed 95 per cent of young people had suffered some form of victimisation (Howard League 2007).

1.5 BREAK

1.6 BREAKING DOWN BARRIERS

Seeing young people as a threat to society creates barriers that affect their relationships with others. Unfortunately many adults do not recognise that continuing to use such stereotypes actually impacts on young people's ability to take on fully their role as citizens.

Shared exercise 1.6: Look the other way

Instructions: Share the scenario below and then discuss briefly the issues that it raises.

David and his girlfriend Lara were no different to any other 15-year-olds in their class. They enjoyed meeting up with their friends and the weekend was a great opportunity to spend time at The Redbush Centre (a local shopping centre). However, after a period of time two boys, whom they knew but were not good friends with, started being rude to other customers and getting into arguments with the security officers at the centre. All those who wore hooded tops were accused of intimidating other customers and generally causing trouble, and were banned from the centre; this included David and Lara. A couple of days later, while waiting for a bus outside the centre, David and Lara were the only people to witness one of the security officers stop a man leaving the store. The officer was asking to see inside a bag the man was holding, when the man hit him in the face, knocking the security officer to the ground. The man ran off.

Question 1: How do you think David and Lara might have reacted?

Question 2: Would it have made any difference if they had been treated more fairly by the security officers and not simply banned from the centre?

A common reaction to being unfairly stereotyped is that individuals withdraw themselves from society; they pull away from it and do not engage with it. This, consequently, limits their ability and willingness to participate and to take on their role as active citizens. However, it is not just the responsibility of adults to ensure good relationships and to look beyond stereotypes. Young people have a responsibility to show that negative perceptions of them are wrong, and that they have a right to be taken seriously as members of their community.

NOTES: 'HOODIES' AND GETTING INVOLVED

Being banned: In May 2005 young people who wore hoodies were banned from entering the Bluewater Shopping Centre in Kent, as the centre's response to antisocial behaviour. This was something that was backed by senior politicians including Tony

Blair, who was prime minister at the time, who said he thought the ban was 'fine and I agree with it' (*The Guardian*, 12/5/05). (A new £200 million shopping centre in Devon repeated such measures. See *BBC News*, 12/3/07.)

A misinformed view: This attitude towards targeting young people based simply on what they wear has angered many, including Lady Sovereign, the rap artist Louise Harman, who led a campaign alongside the release of a single, which presented the other side of the argument:

> I'm fed up with politicians, government people, toffs, people who own shopping centres having a problem with hoodies…being a teenager in Britain, we get targeted for a lot of things. We get all the blame for everything and are looked upon as criminals – that ain't the case most of the time. It's kinda hard being a teenager nowadays because you just get the blame for everything. (*BBC News*, 11/11/05)

Fighting back: In an attempt to prevent this issue marginalising young people, Lady Sovereign found a constructive way to challenge this stereotype and to focus her obvious frustration with the way young people were viewed by adults: through music and a campaign to protect the hoodie, which took her and a petition to Number 10 (see www.savethehoodie.com). It is important that issues like these do not serve to exclude young people from society, but rather, as this example shows, they need to remember their position as citizens and engage in constructive ways to question and challenge the misinformed views of others.

1.7 WHAT IS RESPECT?

Shared exercise 1.7: What's respect?

Instruction 1: To open the discussion, write up the following statement and ask participants to spend 30 seconds or so with those around them, coming up with an answer:

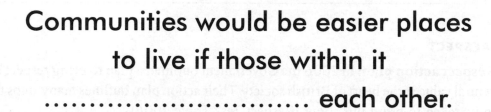

Communities would be easier places to live if those within it .... each other.

Discuss: Get feedback from the groups. An important theme to draw out from discussions is that, to really create a society in which people can live effectively together, individuals need to learn to respect each other. Mutual respect reflects a desire to know and understand each other better. That means looking beyond the stereotypes.

Instruction 2: Following on from your discussion above, start to consider what respect is by using the following quiz.

1. *What do people find most irritating?*

   a) using mobiles without consideration to others (74%)

   b) dropping litter (93%)ANSWER

   c) queue jumping (91%)

2. *Of those who swear in public, how many do not like it when others do the same?*

   a) ¼

   b) ½

   c) ¾ ANSWER

3. *Young people are less annoyed than adults by...*

   a) people who do not say 'please' and 'thank you'

   b) people who do not give up their seat to those who are elderly/pregnant

   c) swearing in public (also people using mobile phones) ANSWER

Discuss: As the quiz may have shown, we all have different levels of tolerance to different types of behaviour. However, when we are living as part of a community it is important that we recognise and learn to respect the feelings of others. Use the following questions to develop your discussion:

1. How do you feel when you are not respected?

2. How do you feel when you are respected?

3. How can you show respect? (Developed in the next section.)

NOTES: RESPECT

Respect action plan: In 2006 the Government outlined a plan to bring respect back as a central value at the heart of British society. Their action plan outlines many steps that need to be taken to bring this about (Respect Task Force 2006).

Keep it simple: However, the issue should not be over-complicated. Developing an ethos of mutual respect demands that individuals try to understand the issues from the perspective of others. By seeing the situation through their eyes, a foundation can be established on which to build stronger, more effective practices and relationships.

Gangs and respect: Recurring gang violence also provides a frightening reminder that respect is not one-way. Headlines such as 'Gangs want respect, so the innocent die' (*The Observer*, 12/8/07), sum up the distorted mentality within these gangs, where their hunt for respect sees them disrespect everyone around them. A one-way expectation of respect is not only unrealistic but also dangerous, and creates communities with greater barriers, where fear is the most potent force, and that desire for individual recognition and understanding is at its least effective.

1.8 SHOWING RESPECT

One way in which you can demonstrate to others you respect them is by listening to what they have to say. Developing your listening skills will not only help to improve your communication with your friends, but also with adults, and will help to break down barriers.

Group exercise 1.8: Communication skills

Instructions: Invite participants to get into groups of three and then to undertake the role of observer, listener or communicator (the group can swap parts between exercises). They will then take part in three different exercises that each demonstrate an aspect of listening. You will need to give them a topic to discuss for each exercise, for example, 'Talk about a time when you have felt disrespected'. It is suggested that each exercise lasts for two minutes. However, this may be too long, particularly for Exercise 1, so may need to be shortened to suit your group.

PART 1 – ROADBLOCKS

Ask the listener and communicator to turn their chairs so that they are back-to-back. The communicator is then to talk for two minutes on a given topic. The listener is to just sit quietly and not respond to the conversation in any way.

Discuss: How did the group find that? How easy was it for the communicator to talk without any encouragement, and how easy was it for the listener to simply sit back and listen? Give them a couple of minutes to discuss.

Points to note: Not being responded to does make it difficult to share a message effectively. There are a number of other barriers, or roadblocks, that can get in the way of effective listening; these include:

- interrupting
- asking multiple questions
- moralising
- blaming
- being indifferent
- patronising
- ignoring.

PART 2 – BODY LANGUAGE

Ask the listener to face the communicator. This time the listener can do anything they can think of to show they are listening, except opening their mouths. The communicator should then speak for two minutes on a given topic.

Discuss: How was the listener able to demonstrate that he/she was listening without speaking?

Points to note: Nonverbal communication, or body language, conveys a significant amount to others. In fact it has been estimated that over 50 per cent of communication takes place this way, compared to around 7 per cent through what we say (for more on this, see Kuhnke 2007). Encouraging body language includes:

- nodding your head
- eye contact
- body position (leaning forward if sitting, arms open, not folded)
- open and interested facial expression.

Negative body language prevents effective communication and increases barriers to building relationships.

PART 3 – OPEN QUESTIONS

Ask the listener to continue to face the communicator. This time the listener is allowed to encourage conversation both verbally and nonverbally. The communicator should speak again for two minutes on a given topic.

Discuss: How was the listener able to encourage conversation verbally?

Points to note: As well as saying 'yes' and 'no', conversations can be encouraged and listening demonstrated through the questions that are asked. Closed questions (questions to which the answer is simply 'yes' or 'no') do not develop conversations. However, by asking questions that begin with the words below, the conversation can be furthered:

- Why?
- What?
- Where?
- When?
- How?

CHALLENGE

Invite the participants to try putting some of these techniques into practice before the next session, and to note the difference that it makes.

1.9 CONCLUSION

1. Review session

This session provides a first step in encouraging you to think about how you want to be seen within your neighbourhoods, as well as how you may be perceived by others. You should have felt challenged to think about how you use stereotypes and to recognise the weaknesses in them. It has introduced the notion of mutual respect and has begun to encourage you to recognise your role in changing attitudes and opinions.

Session outcomes should include participants:

○ working together as a team

○ thinking more about how they are seen when out in their communities

○ being able to recognise stereotypes and the dangers of them

○ recognising specific stereotypes held in relation to young people

○ realising that they have a role to play in breaking down barriers and overturning stereotypes

○ understanding what is meant by mutual respect

○ using listening skills as a means of showing respect.

2. Get some feedback from participants on this first session. Use this as an opportunity to check there are no outstanding questions and worries.

3. Make sure participants know **when the next session is**.

Project ideas

1. Look through newspapers and identify all the stories that mention young people. Classify the stories in relation to the type of story (sport, crime, etc.) and whether they were positive or negative.

2. To counter the negative representation of young people in the press, do some investigative journalism and write a positive story about young people. Then approach your local paper and challenge them to publish it.

3. Search for projects that are trying to challenge assumptions and change attitudes, which will help to improve relationships within communities. Are there any projects like this in your area?

4. Consider constructive ways in which your group can get involved with issues where they feel they are being treated unfairly. For example:

○ put together an action plan full of practical ideas for dealing with an issue at your school or youth group

   o design a campaign (writing petitions, raising awareness – using art and drama)

   o arrange a meeting to talk with key adults (local councillors, MPs, police, teachers).

Helpful websites

- **www.byc.org.uk** – British Youth Council – empowering young people to have a voice

- **www.citizenshipfoundation.org.uk** – see 'Youth Act' and more, on how to effectively engage with your community

- **www.crimeinfo.org.uk** – for facts about crime

- **www.headliners.org** – news articles and comments from young people on issues of importance to them (including stereotypes)

- **www.ipsos-mori.com** – Ipsos MORI – research organisation; look at archive to find results on different social issues

- **www.respect.gov.uk** – UK Home Office plans to encourage respect

- **www.savethehoodie.com** – find out more about the campaign

- **www.youthinformation.com** – National Youth Agency website – more on getting involved as well as other information about crime and justice

References

BBC News (11/11/05) 'Hooray for hoodies', accessed on 3/12/07, www.bbc.co.uk/dorset/content/articles/2005/11/11/hoodies_politics_feature.shtml

BBC News (12/3/07) 'Shopping centre ban on hoodies', accessed on 10/5/08, http://news.bbc.co.uk/go/pr/fr/-/1/hi/england/devon/6442531.stm

Bell, J. (1999) 'Appealing for Justice for Young People: A Critical Analysis of the Crime and Disorder Bill.' In B. Goldson (ed.) *Youth Justice: Contemporary Policy and Practice.* Aldershot: Ashgate.

Brake, M. (1980) *The Sociology of Youth Culture and Youth Subculture.* London: Routledge and Kegan Paul.

Brown, S. (1998) *Understanding Youth Crime.* Buckingham: Open University Press.

Cohen, S. (2002) [1972] *Folk Devils and Moral Panics.* London: Paladin.

Cote, J. (1994) *Adolescent Storm and Stress.* Hove: Erlbaum Associates.

Daily Express (27/2/08) 'Adults to blame for feral gangs says Archbishop'

Daily Mail (16/6/08) 'Don't jail young thugs, give them intensive fostering', accessed on 23/6/08, www.dailymail.co.uk/news/article-1026838/dont-jail-young-thugs-intensive-fostering.html

Daily Mirror (27/5/08) 'It's jail or death for thugs who carry knives says police minister', accessed 23/6/08, www.mirror.co.uk/news/topstories/2008/05/27/it-sjail-or-death-for-thugs-who-carry-knives-says-police-ministe20430918

Guardian, The (12/5/05) 'Blair pledges crackdown on yobs'

Howard League (2007) *Children as Victims: Child-sized Crimes in a Child-sized World.* London: Howard League.

Kuhnke, E. (2007) *Body Language for Dummies.* Chichester: Wiley and Sons Ltd.

Muncie, J. (2004) *Youth Crime: A Critical Introduction.* London: Sage.

Neustatter, A. (1998) 'Kids – what the paper says.' *The Guardian*, 8 April, 8–9.

Observer, The (12/8/07) 'Gangs want respect, so the innocent die'

Pearson, G. (1983) *Hooligans: A History of Respectable Fears.* London: Macmillan.

Porteous, M. and Colston, N. (1980) 'How adolescents are reported in the British Press.' *Journal of Adolescence 3*, 197–207.

Respect Task Force (2006) *Respect Action Plan.* London: Home Office.

Shakespeare, W. (1905) *The Complete Works of Shakespeare.* Oxford: Oxford University Press.

Sun, The (16/6/08) 'Cops give yobs pizza the action', accessed 23/6/08 www.thesun.co.uk/sol/homepage/news/article1295164.ece

Sunday Times, The (20/1/08) 'Sorry Jacqui but your gang handed yobs the get out of jail free card'

Telegraph, The (18/3/08) 'Ed Balls plans baby ASBOs for 10-year-olds', accessed 23/6/08 www.telegraph.co.uk/news/uknews/1581885/Ed-Balls-plans-baby-asbos-for-10-year-olds.html

Session 2

RIGHT AND WRONG

SESSION OVERVIEW

The last session considered the way in which young people see themselves and are seen by others, as well as exploring how the giving and receiving of respect is important in enabling all of us to make the most of our communities. This session aims to take these themes further by encouraging young people to think about their actions: what are the implications or consequences of them? It will help you as a group to consider what makes an act right or wrong and how such meanings are influenced. It will suggest that moral definitions are flexible and that mistakes can be made, which can be particularly easy for young people out on the streets as a result of factors such as lack of knowledge about what the law says, and managing peer pressure.

To help young people identify more clearly what is and is not acceptable, the session will encourage them to focus on feelings. By considering our own feelings and those of others we can more effectively identify responsible behaviour. By looking at the impact of crime on victims, participants will be challenged to question the moral code that they apply within their lives and reflect on what they need to do in order to make the most of the communities they live in.

It is also important to note that the exercises in this session use the foundation of work on listening skills in Session 1. The exercises will provide opportunities for the participants to put these skills into practice, helping to reinforce the importance of communication as a means of giving and receiving respect.

Aims

- to build on themes considered in Session 1
- to encourage young people to think about their actions while out in their communities
- to consider what makes an action right or wrong
- to consider the importance of recognising our own feelings and those of others

Session 2 timed outline

ACTION	TIME IN MINUTES	DESCRIPTION	RESOURCES	NOTES
1. Introduction	10	ask participants to read and sign statements (see Section 2) • welcome • refresh ground rules • re-cap Session 1 • introduce Session 2	2.1a 2.1b 2.1c 2.1d	
2. Is it right or wrong fixed or flexible?	20	This section encourages you to think about the meanings that we give our actions. See handout and: • share findings • contrast with statements signed on arrival. Note how right and wrong is flexible, with different meanings being linked to different factors and different times and places. Meaning is impacted by 'where, when, who, what and how'.	2.2	
3. The ingredients – What makes something right or wrong?	10	Different people can bring different meanings to actions. See bullying exercise. 1. How easy was it to reach an answer? 2. How many different points of view? 3. What caused the different opinions? A definition suspends the impact of different factors. However, knowing what these definitions are, particularly in the context of the criminal law, is not always easy.	2.3	
4. Break	5			

Session 2 timed outline *continued*

ACTION	TIME IN MINUTES	DESCRIPTION	RESOURCES	NOTES
5. Feelings	15	Reflecting on our feelings and the feelings of others can help us to reduce the mistakes that we make. In pairs ask participants to refresh listening skills. 1. What does it mean to feel safe and unsafe? 2. What makes them feel like this? 3. If you felt like this, what would you do next? A feeling of safety encourages us to be more involved in our communities. It is important that we recognise that our right to feel safe comes with the responsibility to make sure others feel safe too.		
6. Recognising other people's feelings	25	Young people can often be victims of crimes. ● See Sheet 2.6a. *Discuss*: How might the victims feel? ● See Sheet 2.6b. *Discuss*: Reflect on victims' reactions Words alone can have an impact on others. ● See 'Words will never hurt me' exercise and facilitator's notes.	2.6a 2.6b 2.6c 2.6d	
7. Conclusion	5	1. Review session and reflect on outcomes. 2. Provide information for participants on accessing support. 3. Check time of next session.		

- to consider the impact of crime on victims

- to recognise that we have both the right to be safe and the responsibility to make sure others feel safe too.

Objectives

Session outcomes will include participants:

- developing listening skills

- recognising the complex nature of right and wrong

- having a growing awareness of what makes an action right or wrong

- being able to reflect on the link between feelings and actions

- recognising the impact of actions on others.

2.1 INTRODUCTION TO SESSION 2

Welcome

1. As participants arrive, put them into groups of about four people. Distribute the four statement sheets (2.1a, 2.1b, 2.1c, 2.1d) and ask participants to read and sign them. Then collect the sheets and start the session.

2. Welcome the participants back and do a quick check on names (if needed).

3. Remind the participants of the ethos of the programme, and particularly that the more they put in to the course, the more they will get out of it – so think openly about the issues, discuss them honestly and enjoy them!

4. Refresh your ground rules.

5. Re-cap themes from Session 1. Remind the participants of some of the issues you addressed within Session 1, which will have included them:

    *   working together as a team

    *   thinking more about how they are seen when out in their communities

    *   being able to recognise stereotypes and the dangers of them

    *   recognising specific stereotypes held in relation to young people

    *   realising that they have a role to play in breaking down barriers and overturning stereotypes

    *   understanding what is meant by mutual respect

    *   using listening skills as a means of showing respect.

    Ask for feedback or thoughts following on from the last session.

Introduce Session 2

This course is about giving you the knowledge and skills that will enable you to make the most of the communities that you live in. Session 1 looked at the way in which young people are seen by others and the importance of developing an attitude of mutual respect. Part of this involves people understanding and being aware of the impact of their actions. This session, therefore, will ask you to think about your actions and how they impact on the way in which you are seen. Are your actions right or wrong? How do you know? Who defines what you should and should not do? Knowing what is and is not acceptable is not always straightforward. However, by looking at these issues through considering our 'feelings' can make them easier to understand. This will include thinking about the impact of actions on victims. What is important is that by the end of the session you will recognise that we all have a right to feel safe and a responsibility to make sure others feel safe too. The outline of this session is as follows:

1. Introduction to Session 2
2. Is right and wrong fixed or flexible?
3. The ingredients – What makes something right or wrong?
4. Break
5. Feelings
6. Recognising other people's feelings
7. Conclusion to Session 2.

Sheet 2.1a

Using another person's identity		
RIGHT	WRONG	IT DEPENDS

Sheet 2.1b

Killing someone		
RIGHT	WRONG	IT DEPENDS

Sheet 2.1c

Stealing medicine from a hospital		
RIGHT	WRONG	IT DEPENDS

Giving out drugs

RIGHT	WRONG	IT DEPENDS

2.2 IS RIGHT AND WRONG FIXED OR FLEXIBLE?

What is right and what is wrong? Are moral meanings fixed, or can they change? The following section will invite you to think about different actions and the meanings that you give to them. Are acts that involve lying, hurting others, taking something from others and behaving antisocially always wrong?

Group exercise 2.2: Right or wrong?

Instructions: Hand out Sheet 2.2. Ask the groups to try to answer the questions. You may wish to get them to look at the questions in a different order, making sure all questions are covered.

DO EXERCISE.

Discuss:

1. Ask each group to share their findings. How did the different factors impact on the way in which they saw the actions? Explore whether there were different opinions and what those differences were.

   Then:

2. Ask participants to reflect on their earlier answers concerning the following acts:

   a) Using another person's identity

   b) Killing someone

   c) Stealing medicine from a hospital

   d) Giving out drugs.

   Have views stayed the same or have they changed? How many recognised that a particular set of circumstances could legitimise all of these actions – from a soldier killing someone during a war, to a pharmacist handing over prescribed drugs?

The point of this exercise is to show that right and wrong is not fixed, but that it changes as a result of different factors – circumstances such as:

- **where** the action takes place
- **when** the action takes place
- **who** is involved
- **what** the intended aim of the action is
- **how** it is perceived/made sense of (by you and others).

SCENARIOS: IS RIGHT AND WRONG FIXED OR FLEXIBLE?

Look at the following scenarios and consider whether you think the act is right, wrong or 'it depends', and why.

1. Lying

a. You have brought your mum a birthday present. As you walk into the house she sees you, so you hide the present behind your back. She asks what it is and you say, 'Oh, it's nothing, it is for a drama project at school.'

b. You want to get in to see an 18 film; you are only 16, but when asked you tell them that it was your eighteenth birthday two weeks ago.

c. As you leave the supermarket you realise you have only paid for one of the two drinks you are holding. You are stopped as you leave and asked if you have paid for both drinks. You say 'yes'.

2. Hurting others

a. You are outside a local youth club arguing with another person about football teams. Suddenly they try to hit you. You push the other person away and they fall and bang their head.

b. You are in the park with friends. You see some younger people from your school, and for a laugh you decide to rugby-tackle one of them, knocking them flat onto the ground.

c. You are in a sports match; you are chasing the ball. To get it, you push another person out of the way.

3. Taking something

a. You take a handful of sweets worth only 10p from a pick-and-mix counter and do not pay for them.

b. You see a £10 note lying in the street. You try and find the owner, but when you can't, you take the money.

c. You take your next-door-neighbour's bike without asking. A few hours later you bring it back.

4. Being antisocial

a. You play football against the wall of a house, even though you know the person that lives there does not like it.

b. You meet up with some friends outside the local supermarket and spend time talking and laughing and just having fun.

c. You buy some alcohol with friends with the intention of getting drunk in the park.

NOTES: CHANGING ATTITUDES TO CAPITAL PUNISHMENT

The changing nature of right and wrong: The fact is that notions of right and wrong are not fixed; they change through time and space. Different periods of history reflect these changes and show the transient nature of notions of right and wrong. Within society, laws provide a means of defining what is seen to be morally acceptable. (We will return to the law in more detail in Session 3.) However, even laws change over time, and differ between countries. Capital punishment is a state-sanctioned response to crime, which sees the taking of the offender's life as an acceptable punishment for their actions. Consider the cases of Joseph Wood and Thomas Underwood, and that of Atefah Sahaaleh:

- **In 1791** 14-year-olds **Joseph Wood** and **Thomas Underwood** found themselves before a judge for robbing a 12-year-old child. They were frequent visitors to court for their behaviour, but this time they had gone too far. An account said:

  > so often had they been arraigned at the bar…that the judge declared…it was necessary for the public safety to cut them off, in order that other boys might learn that, inured [accustomed] to wickedness, their tender age would not save them from an ignominious fate. (Rayner and Crook 1926: 187)

So that others could learn, and to stop their offending behaviour, these two boys were executed.

- **In 2004** a 16-year-old girl, **Atefah Sahaaleh**, found herself before a judge, accused of 'crimes against chastity' – behaving in a way seen as unacceptable for a woman. In the past she had been arrested for being at a party and being in a car alone with a boy. But being caught in an abusive relationship with a 51-year-old man, and facing a petition that suggested she was a 'terrible influence on local schoolgirls' (*BBC News*, 27/7/06), resulted in a death sentence being passed on her. The Iranian Supreme Court declared that the 'execution will take place in public…so that the public may learn from it' (Amnesty International 2007: 15). Atefah was hanged.

From accepted to rejected: Despite the 200 years that separate these two cases, it still appears that there are a number of similarities, such as that all three young people were deemed a threat and executed so that others would learn. (See Session 1 on stereotypes.) However, attitudes towards such executions alter dramatically. In 1791, under English law, Joseph and Thomas were two of many young people who suffered this fate; their deaths would not have been regarded as extraordinary. Atefah's death, on the other hand, came at a time when fewer countries still used capital punishment, and even less condoned it for those under the age of 18 years. As a result, Atefah's death became the subject of a documentary by the BBC, as well as a case highlighted by Amnesty International to challenge the actions of the Iranian government and express outrage at what had happened. (To find out more about capital punishment, see the website links at the end of the session.)

2.3 THE INGREDIENTS – WHAT MAKES SOMETHING RIGHT OR WRONG?

As we have seen, the flexible nature of right and wrong means that it is possible for different people to give different meaning to the same action. Not only is this meaning shaped by *here   hen   ho   ha* (see Section 2.2), but also by *ho   we* as individuals make sense of the action based on our own background and experiences. We look at this in the next exercise.

Group exercise 2.3: Bullying

Bullying affects many people at some time in their lives. Although it is hard to say exactly how many of us are bullied, research suggests that it could be as many as one in three (Office of the Children's Commissioner, 2006). Why are so many people victims of bullying when we are all aware that it is wrong? The problem lies in the way we see bullying.

Instructions: Split participants into groups. Give groups the Sheet 2.3 and ask them to state when they think Peter is being bullied.

DO EXERCISE.

Discuss: Reflect on the group's findings, using the questions below if helpful. Focus on any differences within the groups as they reached their answers – considering particularly how individual experiences and understandings of bullying influenced opinions.

1. How easy it was for them to reach an answer with which they were all happy?

2. How many different points of view were there in the group?

3. What might influence individual opinions? (Answers may include: upbringing, culture, beliefs, social status, self-esteem, education, personal experiences.)

In reality the freedom to define the nature of one's actions means that behaviour that negatively affects others can go unrecognised, and is even accepted as part of everyday life. This can happen with bullying, where both bullied and bullies come to see bullying as normal, just something that happens.

A definition

Question: What difference would it have made if you had done the exercise with the following definition in front of you?

> Bullying is deliberate one-off or regular acts, intended to hurt or intimidate another at home, school, work or out in the streets.

A definition makes us overlook the factors that impact on the way we consider an action and lead us quickly and easily to make a judgement on whether that action is right or wrong. This is exactly the same out on the streets, where the criminal law provides definitions as to what behaviour is or is not acceptable, and therefore what is right and wrong. (See Session 3.) The problem is that we don't always know these definitions or carry round guidance on what they are. So we need a method that helps us take responsibility for our actions, so that we can act in a way that encourages respect for others. To do this, we need to think about feelings. (Distribute Sheet 2.3: Bullying.)

BULLYING

Look at the following example. In which case does your group think that Peter is actually being bullied?

1. Peter, against his will, is pushed by others.

2. Peter, against his will, is REGULARLY pushed by others.

3. Peter, against his will, is regularly pushed by others AT SCHOOL.

4. Peter, against his will, is regularly pushed by others at school who are OLDER than him.

5. Peter, against his will, is regularly pushed by others at school who are older than him, BECAUSE he is small for his age.

NOTES

Defining right and wrong: There are many different philosophical positions in relation to morality, stretching back through history (for overview see Thompson 2005). These have seen right and wrong defined by gods, kings, parliaments and societies. However, it is only more recently that it has been acknowledged that the individual plays a significant part in this process (see MacIntyre 1966). It is now recognised that individuals themselves can construct moral meanings as a consequence of the experiences they have been through. The implications of this are that consideration needs to be given to the context within which actions are carried out. This does not mean that young people can get away with saying that they did not know that what they had done was wrong, but that adults should accept that mistakes can be made. There is also a greater responsibility for both adults and young people to be better educated as to what is and is not acceptable. By growing in awareness not only of what the laws says, but also of how certain actions affect others within the community, we gain useful information which helps individuals make decisions about whether their actions are right or wrong.

Gangs: Within 'gangs' a culture can develop where the moral meanings accepted by its members can be very different from those held by other people within the community, or country as a whole. Take the best-known international example – the Mafia. In the following rather graphic account that details the life of one particular New York member of the Mafia, the author explains what it is that sets certain individuals out to be successful gangsters.

> By birth, certainly, they were not prepared in any way to achieve their desires. They were not the smartest kids in the neighbourhood. They were not born the richest. They weren't even the toughest. In fact they lacked almost all the necessary talents that might have helped them to satisfy the appetites of their dreams, except one – their talent for violence. Violence was natural to them. It fuelled them. Snapping a man's arm, cracking his ribs with an inch-and-a-half-diameter lead pipe, slamming his fingers in the door of a car, or casually taking his life was entirely acceptable. It was routine. A familiar exercise. (Peleggi 1985: 42–43)

In order to fulfil the role of a gangster, an individual had to develop a separate sense of right and wrong in which acts of extreme violence were seen as a 'normal' part of everyday life. This distorted moral code formed alongside the individual's self-centred preoccupation with achieving status and a particular reputation, in the context of a culture in which violence was an integral part. As we considered in Session 1, this provides another perverse example of how a desire to be 'respected' is rooted in a lack of respect or concern for others.

2.4 BREAK

2.5 FEELINGS

To help reduce the likelihood of us attaching the 'wrong' meaning to our actions and to promote mutual respect within our community, it is important that we develop the skill of thinking about what we do based on the way we feel and the way we might make others feel.

Shared exercise 2.5: Feelings

Instructions 1: Take time to refresh listening skills (see Session 1) if needed. Ask participants, in pairs, to find out how each other is feeling today. They are not to take one word for an answer; the idea is to see how much they can get out of the other person through using good, open questions and listening effectively.

Instructions 2: Continuing in pairs, ask groups to express in words:

a) what it means to feel safe and unsafe

b) what could make them feel safe or unsafe

c) what they might do next if they felt either way.

Discuss: Consider the contrasting views about the differences between feeling safe and unsafe, and highlight the answers on a flipchart. Some participants may find it hard to express their feelings, but they can always try and look at the issues from someone else's point of view.

Examine findings in answers to question c): When people feel safe they are far more likely to look out for others and be able to enjoy the world around them – in contrast to when they feel unsafe, which can hamper 'their ability to make a positive contribution' (Office of the Children's Commissioner 2006). This highlights the fact that ensuring that people feel safe is important for creating an atmosphere that encourages the giving and receiving of respect in communities.

Everyone has the right to feel safe within his or her community and we all have the responsibility to make sure that everyone is able to feel like this. Asking ourselves whether our actions make us and those around us feel safe or unsafe can help us know what is right and wrong, out on the streets.

You can use this table to illustrate how considering our feelings can serve as a moral guide.

Action	You feel:	Others feel:	Acceptability	Right or wrong?
Kicking football against shop window	safe (with friends and having fun)	unsafe (People in shop feel intimidated and are anxious about whether you will do anything else.)	not acceptable	wrong
[Invite groups to add their own examples…]				

NOTES: KNIVES

Carrying a knife is a good example of where different people can attach different moral meanings to the same action. For some young people, maybe as many as one in three (*The Observer*, 18/5/08), carrying a knife is linked with self-defence, the need to feel safe, and on that basis it is justified and seen as acceptable. However, for many others, both adults and young people alike, the association between knives and the potential for serious injury leads to fear and to feeling unsafe out on the streets, impacting on where they go and what they do. Parliament has taken the view that carrying weapons, even for self-defence, is against the law (you may wish to contrast this with gun laws in the USA), and indeed there are moves to strengthen these laws. But if young people really do justify carrying a knife in order to feel safe (for some it may be more about social status – see discussion on gun crime in Session 3), then surely this suggests the need to pay more attention to how adults can help young people feel safe on the streets, so that individuals don't feel the need to carry knives. All young people have the right to feel safe, but this brings with it the responsibility to think about others and to make sure they feel safe too; carrying a knife is not the answer. To find the answer, barriers between young people and adults need to be broken down and conversations need to take place, in which as mutual partners both groups can learn to understand the issues from the other's perspective, laying a foundation for effective action. Discuss…

2.6 RECOGNISING OTHER PEOPLE'S FEELINGS

Two of the most frequent crimes that young victims face are assault and theft or robbery. Look at (or listen to) the following accounts and consider how these young people might have felt as a result of their experience.

Exercise 2.6: Victims (1)

Instructions: This exercise can be done in groups or as a shared discussion. Read out, or give groups Sheet 2.6a. Then discuss. Following this, hand out Sheet 2.6b. Read, then discuss.

Discuss 1: How do you think the victims might have felt as a result of their experience? Consider their emotional reaction to these two true accounts, and which parts of the incident had particular significance. (Sheet 2.6b provides an account of a reaction to these incidents.)

Discuss 2: After reading Sheet 2.6b, how did this compare to what the group discussed earlier? Are they surprised by the findings? What effect did the circumstances of the incidents have in terms of impact on the victim?

Common reactions from victims include shock, fear, guilt, anger and a loss of self-confidence. It is also important to recognise that the same crime can affect individuals in very different ways. For example, for one person having their watch stolen may not be too distressing, whereas for another the watch may hold strong emotional meaning or memories, leaving the victim very distressed. The power of a crime's emotional impact should never be underestimated.

EXERCISE 2.6: VICTIMS – THE INCIDENT

Assault – Part 1

I was walking home one night across a bridge and saw two lads pulling at a student's scarf. I walked out onto the bridge, and on seeing me they left him alone, but all I had done was give them a new target: me. They asked me where I was from and whether I had any money. When I said I had no money they slammed me up against a wall and one of them headbutted me, while the other one held me. They tried to drag me down an alley to beat me up. But I was able to get away.

Robbery – Part 1

Me and my friend were on our way back from school. She didn't want to cut through the field but I said it would be okay. Anyway, this boy just went running past and grabbed my bag. I thought about running after him, but I was really scared because he was a lot bigger than me. The bag had my CD player and everything in it. I'd only had the new picture phone a week… I didn't think really, I just grabbed it out of my pocket. I kept snapping as he ran away. (Victim Support 2003: 7)

EXERCISE 2.6: VICTIMS – THE IMPACT

Assault – Part 2

I went to check on the student, but he was so frightened by what had happened he could not even get the words out of his mouth. I went home, wanting to get my friends so that we could go back and deal with them, angry that these people had tried to attack me. Even though I had been able to deal with it, when I sat down on my own that night I felt uneasy, nervous, and yes, I felt scared. For months after the feeling of fear did not go away; the smell of alcohol was enough to trigger a memory and thoughts of what could have happened. I was more cautious about being out at night and I have never forgotten the reaction of the student and the realisation that such behaviour can affect people so much.

Robbery – Part 2

I was really upset to start with. I felt really stupid because I was the one who said it would be okay. I was sad that my bag had been taken and it made me angry when I thought about all the stuff that was in it, especially the CD player that I had been saving up for ages to have. All this really knocked my confidence for a bit, not only talking with people at school but also with going out. However, even though I started off feeling quite powerless, when I was able to show people, like the police, the photos of what had happened, I started to feel in control again. At least he hadn't completely got away with it.

'WORDS WILL NEVER HURT ME'?

The saying 'Sticks and stones may break my bones, but words will never hurt me' suggests that you can expect to be injured as a result of physical violence, but that words just do not hurt. However, this is not true: the power of the tongue should not be underestimated, for words can cause serious damage.

Exercise: Victims (2)

Instructions: Either in groups or as a shared discussion, hand out or read out Sheet 2.6c and consider the questions. Use Sheet 2.6d to help you in discussing the issues raised in the questions.

It is important that we as members of our community do think about how our actions might affect others. We may not always get this right, but we do have a responsibility to do all we can to make sure others feel safe. Only then can we claim the right to feel safe ourselves. Note that the most common factor associated with being a victim is being an offender!

NOTES: VICTIMS

Young people can be victims: In Session 1 the notion of young people as a threat was considered, and a stereotype that has emerged in which young people are seen as either active or potentially active offenders. However, one report in 2007 suggested that 95 per cent of children are victims on at least one occasion (Howard League 2007). Seventy per cent of those victims said that they had been hit or kicked, and just under half were called racist names. These findings reflect other research, which suggests that young people 'are more sinned against than sinning' (Hartless *et al.* 1995).

It just happens: Feelings such as shock, fear, guilt, anger and a loss of security are common amongst victims (Victim Support Norfolk 2007) and often people will need support in managing these feelings as part of making sense of what has happened to them. One of the major concerns about young people as victims is that these crimes never get reported, leaving many young victims without the support that they deserve (90% of young victims reported feeling distressed after the crime (Morgan and Zender 1992)). Cause for concern is that one of the reasons why young people do not seek help is because they themselves do not define what has happened to them as a 'crime', as was shown in a study on violent attacks, in which half of the young victims simply saw the incident as something that 'just happened'. Only a few of all the young people interviewed saw the attack against them as a crime (Aye Maung 1995).

Letting people know: This problem is further compounded by fears young people have over the way peers and adults may react to hearing about the incident. In relation to peers, these fears relate to being labelled a sneak or becoming the focus of retaliation, whereas in relation to adults, particularly the police, the fears relate to not being listened to, not being believed and not wanting to waste time. (See Victim Support Norfolk 2007 for a useful overview of relationships between young people and police.) When young people do feel comfortable enough to talk, they are most likely to speak with parents, followed by their friends and then their teachers (Victim Support Norfolk 2007); friends have a very important role to play. It is worth making sure that young people know how to access support if they do become a victim of crime, or find themselves talking with someone who has.

'WORDS WILL NEVER HURT ME'

This is an account from a taxi driver:

> I was on the rank and they started attacking my vehicle. All of a sudden the racial abuse started: 'You black so-and-so, you Paki so-and-so, etc.' Quite a few of them got together and there were a few taxi drivers trying to stop it all and managed to defuse the situation there. But within a few minutes they were back again; kicking the vehicle, punching it, everything – 'You Paki so-and-so, we're gonna get you.' (Victim Support 2006: 49)

Question 1: How do you think the taxi driver may have felt after this experience?

Question 2: Who else might be affected by this abuse, particularly if it took place in the driver's street?

Question 3: What other effect might these types of attacks have on someone?

'WORDS WILL NEVER HURT ME' – FACILITATOR'S NOTES

This is an account from a taxi driver:

> I was on the rank and they started attacking my vehicle. All of a sudden the racial abuse started: 'You black so-and-so, you Paki so-and-so, etc.' Quite a few of them got together and there were a few taxi drivers trying to stop it all and managed to defuse the situation there. But within a few minutes they were back again; kicking the vehicle, punching it, everything – 'You Paki so-and-so, we're gonna get you.' (Victim Support 2006: 49)

Question 1: How do you think the taxi driver may have felt after this experience?
The most common reactions to hate crime are anger, fear and hurt.

Question 2: Who else might be affected by this abuse, particularly if it took place in the driver's street?
This behaviour can impact on members of the family, and often parents worry about the effect on their children.

'We have developed a terrible sense of insecurity, but the worst of all is my little one. Since the last attack he wakes up almost every night with nightmares, crying…' (Victim Support 2006: 51). (This parent had suffered from various attacks, including bricks being thrown through the window.)

Question 3: What other effect might these types of attacks have on someone?
Other impacts of this type of crime include different types of illness, including depression and other physical problems. It might also impact financially on victims, who, through fear or as the result of loss or damage, are not able to earn or save what they need.

'I thought if I was going to get harassed when I go out, then I'd rather stay inside. It got to the point where I stopped working and I started claiming benefits' (Victim Support 2006: 51).

2.7 CONCLUSION

1. **Review session**

   This session has shown how important it is for us to take personal responsibility for our actions. The boundaries of what is right and wrong can shift in different contexts, and we must be aware of that in recognising what is and is not acceptable within our communities. By reflecting on feelings it is possible to get a clearer idea of what behaviour promotes mutual respect, and as a result fosters communities in which people feel safe.

   The session outcomes should include participants:

   o developing listening skills

   o recognising the complex nature of right and wrong

   o having a growing awareness of what makes an action right or wrong

   o being able to reflect on the link between feelings and actions

   o recognising the impact of their actions on others.

2. **Check all are okay**

   In view of the nature of the material discussed, do make sure that individuals within the group are okay. If issues that have been raised within the session have affected them, make sure they know who to turn to and what to do. You will find helpful web addresses below.

3. **Date of the next session**

Project ideas

1. Develop a campaign to make sure other young people know how to access support if they are bullied or find themselves a victim of crime, particularly if this happens when they are out on the streets.

2. Check out what anti-bullying measures are in place at your school, youth club or anywhere else you spend time with other young people. Is it doing its job, and if it isn't, what can you do to improve it?

3. Do a crime survey and find out whether your area has a problem with young people being involved in crime. If you do identify trouble areas in your community, let adults such as headteachers and the police know about it, and see whether together you can change it.

Helpful websites

- **www.amnesty.org.uk** – Amnesty International – human rights campaigning organisation

- **www.are-you-ok.org.uk** – Victim Support's site for young people

- **www.bbc.co.uk/religion/ethics/capitalpunishment** – more on capital punishment

- **www.bullying.co.uk** – Bullying UK website – information on bullying. See also Kidscape and NSPCC

- **www.childline.org.uk** – or phone for confidential support and advice: 0800 1111

- **www.crimeinfo.org.uk** – for facts about crime

- **www.deathpenalty.org** – Death Penalty Focus – focuses on death penalty in United States of America

- **www.11million.org.uk** – site for the Children's Commissioner for England

- **www.victimsupport.org.uk** – main site for Victim Support

- **www.worldcoalition.org** – World Coalition against the Death Penalty – working against the death penalty throughout the world

REFERENCES

Amnesty International (2007) *Iran: The Last Executioner of Children*. London: Amnesty International.

Aye Maung, N. (1995) *Young People, Victimisation and the Police*. Home Office Research Study No. 140. London: HMSO.

BBC News (27/7/06) 'Execution of a teenage girl', accessed on 15/1/08, http://news.bbc.co.uk/go/pr/fr/-/1/hi/programmes/5217424.stm

Hartless, J., Ditton, J., Nair, G. and Phillips, S. (1995) 'More sinned against than sinning: a study of young teenagers' experience of crime.' *British Journal of Criminology 35*, 1, 114–133.

Howard League (2007) *Children as Victims: Child-sized Crimes in a Child-Sized World*. London: Howard League.

MacIntyre, A. (1966) *A Short History of Ethics*. London: Routledge.

Morgan, J. and Zender, L. (1992) *Child Victims: Crime, Impact and Criminal Justice*. Oxford: Clarendon Press.

Observer, The (18/5/08) 'One in three back carrying knives.'

Office of the Children's Commissioner (2006) *Bullying Today*. London: Office of the Children's Commissioner.

Peleggi, N. (1985) *Wiseguy*. London: Corgi Books.

Rayner, J. and Crook, G. (1926) *The Complete Newgate Calendar*. London: Navarre Society.

Thompson, M. (2005) *Ethical Theory*. Coventry: Hodder Murray.

Victim Support (2003) *Annual Review 2003*. London: Victim Support National Office.

Victim Support (2006) *Crime and Prejudice. The Support Needs of Victims of Hate Crime: A Research Report*. London: Victim Support National Office.

Victim Support Norfolk (2007) *The Support Needs of Young Victims of Crime: A Research Report*. Norwich: Victim Support Norfolk.

Session 3

IT'S A CRIME

SESSION OVERVIEW

The last session looked at the flexible nature of morality and the factors that can impact on the moral meanings that we give to our actions. This session starts by revisiting these themes and considers them within the specific context of peer pressure. It challenges young people to make a stand, suggesting communication skills that might help them achieve this effectively. The session goes on to look at the point and purpose of laws themselves, identifying that at its best the law looks to provide a framework within which individuals can live peacefully. Of course the role of the criminal law is to define what society sees as acceptable and unacceptable. However, even though there is an expectation of young people to know what the law says – do they? The point is that the law covers a massive range of behaviours and it is very complex, so that it is not possible for young people to know exactly what it says. This means that it is also important to rely on approaches such as that demonstrated in Session 2, where actions are considered with regard to feeling safe or unsafe, from which a moral conclusion can be drawn. Session 3 finishes by, first, reminding the group that crime also has an impact on offenders, and going on to suggest that the role of enforcing the law is not simply for those who are paid to do it, but a responsibility for all of us.

The session continues to encourage the group in developing communication skills, reinforcing the importance of these as a tool in actively demonstrating respect.

Aims

- to consider peer pressure

- to explore the purpose of the criminal law

- to raise awareness of the extent of the criminal law

- to raise awareness of particular criminal offences

- to consider the impact of crime on offenders

- to develop communication skills through practice.

Session 3 timed outline

ACTION	TIME IN MINUTES	DESCRIPTION	RESOURCES	NOTES
1. Introduction	5	• welcome • refresh ground rules • re-cap Session 2 • introduce Session 3	Flipchart	
2. Putting forward your point	12	Our understanding of what is right and wrong can be greatly influenced by others. • consider what peer pressure is • why do our friends have such an impact on us? Standing up to peer pressure is not easy. By developing the way in which we communicate a message, we can more effectively stand up to peer pressure. • An 'I' message: 'When you…I feel…because…'		
3. The point of the criminal law	20	In groups: 1. You are in a community with no rules. What would it be like? Who would be the winners and losers? 2. Discuss and then present an argument for the four laws your group believes to be the most important. The criminal law provides a means of creating order and protecting the peace.		
4. Break	5			

Session 3 timed outline *continued*

ACTION	TIME IN MINUTES	DESCRIPTION	RESOURCES	NOTES
5. Spot the crime	25	A crime is an action that is harmful to us or others and an act, if committed, that the state will punish. The law covers many areas – See exercise. It can be hard to identify what makes an offence. 1. Attempt 'Spot the crime' exercise. 2. Reflect on answers to exercise. The complex nature of the law makes it important to keep reflecting on how our actions might affect others, preventing a breach of the peace.	Table 3.5 3.5a 3.5b	
6. Impact of crime on the offender	12	It is necessary to recognise that crime impacts on offenders as well as victims. See case studies. Discuss the impact of being an offender, particularly on relationships.	3.6	
7. Enforcing the law	6	The point of the criminal law is to keep people safe. 1. Who should enforce the criminal law? We all have a responsibility to enforce the criminal law. 2. Why are the police important to help enforce the law? The police have particular powers to act on behalf of the state to maintain social order.		
8. Conclusion	5	1. Review session and reflect on outcomes. 2. Remind participants how they can go about reporting a crime. 3. Check time of next session.		

Outcomes

Session outcomes will include participants:

- considering effective communication and making a stand
- recognising the point and purpose of the criminal law
- understanding the range and complexity of the criminal law
- recognising the impact of crime on an offender
- realising that we all have responsibility to enforce the criminal law.

3.1 INTRODUCTION TO SESSION 3

Welcome

1. Welcome the participants back and do a quick check on names (if needed).

2. Refresh your ground rules.

3. Re-cap themes from Session 2. Remind the participants of some of the issues you addressed within Session 2, which will have included them:

   ○ developing listening skills

   ○ recognising the complex nature of right and wrong

   ○ having a growing awareness of what makes an action right or wrong

   ○ being able to reflect on the link between feelings and actions

   ○ recognising the impact of actions on others.

   Ask for feedback on whether anyone has thought about these themes in between sessions.

Introduce Session 3

Knowing what is right and wrong is one thing, standing up for it is another. The session starts by asking you to think a bit about how our friends can influence the meanings that we give our actions and how easy (or difficult) it is to make a stand against them. After looking at some practical skills that can help us with sharing a message, we go on to look at the point and purpose of the criminal law, which we learn, at its best, is there to ensure that all of us are able to live in peace. You will get a chance to demonstrate your knowledge of the law, and also to think about the impact of crime on offenders, and whose role it is to enforce the law. An outline of this session is as follows:

1. Introduction to Session 3
2. Putting forward your point
3. The point of the criminal law
4. Break
5. Spot the crime
6. Impact of crime on the offender
7. Enforcing the law
8. Conclusion to Session 3.

3.2 PUTTING FORWARD YOUR POINT

In the last session we saw how individuals are involved in shaping what they see as right and wrong. The result is that different people and groups can have different ideas on what is and is not acceptable. Young people may see these different attitudes when they compare what may be acceptable at home with family to what is acceptable when out in the neighbourhood with friends. Our friends can greatly influence the way we think about actions as right or wrong.

Shared exercise 3.2: Peer pressure

Instructions: Simply read out the statements and discuss.

A view from a 10-year-old (1)

Say I am with my friends and they're daring me to do something wrong and they're insulting me and calling me a chicken, I would do it – because I don't want to lose friends. People I've hung out with in the park have said if you don't do something, that's really naughty, you can't ever play with us again. I'd really try to see if I could do it, I would go to lots of trouble. (Frankel 2006: 124)

Discuss 1: Ask the group if they can relate to any of the comments made above. How has peer pressure affected members of the group? Does the way peer pressure affect you change, as you get older?

A view from a 10-year-old (2)

[Two boys were talking about throwing stones at the windows of a house.]

At the time when I was with my friends I would probably not know that it was wrong, because I was probably just having fun with them, you're having a laugh, until something bad happens, when you realise it is wrong. (Frankel 2006: 125)

Discuss 2: Why do our friends have such an influence on the meaning we give to some of our actions? The example above suggests that the desire to be accepted by our friends is very important, to the point that it can lead to us changing the meaning we give actions – in this case from being wrong to a bit of fun. (The notes on pp.76–77 provide more on peer pressure.)

Standing up to peer pressure can be difficult for both adults and young people, as it often requires us to question or challenge the point of view of others. Challenging another's opinions can very easily cause conflict. However, the actual way in which we communicate a message can have a dramatic effect on how other people respond to it.

Group exercise 3.2: Effective communication

Instructions: Consider what makes communication effective. Proceed to look at an 'I' message. Then invite groups to try giving an 'I' message in response to the question below. The facilitator (if you feel comfortable) could act out two different ways of trying to communicate a message, using as a guide the points below.

DO:

- stay calm
- be respectful
- listen to the other person

DO NOT:

- *raise your voice*
- patronise the other person
- ignore the other person

'I' message

An 'I message' provides a less confrontational way of expressing and sharing feelings with others. Here is an outline of how to give an 'I message':

1. **'When you'** – explain what it is that the other person may have done.

2. **'...I feel'** – far less aggressive than 'you make me' which is immediately confrontational, resulting in others becoming defensive.

3. **...because** – of the impact that it has, or might have.

Example: '*When you* speak to me like that, *I feel* scared and upset, *because* I feel that I deserve to be treated with more respect than that.'

Question:

Your friend wants you to buy a pirated DVD. You do not think pirated DVDs are right because you have heard they are linked to organised crime. Your friend starts to get angry with you, calling you a coward. This upsets you. Respond to your friend using an 'I message'.

NOTES: FACING UP TO PEER PRESSURE – WILLIAM WILBERFORCE

Peer pressure stems from a desire in us to belong, to demonstrate our similarity to others. As a result of wanting to promote a positive image to our peers we can easily find ourselves behaving in ways that we would never even consider in front of others, like our families. This need to be accepted by our peers puts us at risk of making mistakes in our effort to impress. Peer pressure is not just a problem in the teenage years; it remains a problem no matter what age you are.

Making a stand against one's parents is a regular occurrence for many young people. But making a stand against one's friends, one's peers, is not as common or as easy. Standing up to our peers means reflecting an image of ourselves onto others, an image that will come to shape the way we are seen and consequently the extent to which we are included in what goes on around us. It is therefore easier to follow, to join in and not to question. However, this can lead to the continuing use of unfair stereotypes, bullying, and a group culture in which certain acts become accepted, although those same acts in relation to others would be seen as unacceptable, even against the law. To stand up and to challenge one's peers is hard, but when it makes the difference between others being safe or unsafe, then it must be done.

William Wilberforce is a great historical example of someone who stood up against his peers, and in so doing changed attitudes and opinions that had lasted for millennia, and altered the lives of many by abolishing the transatlantic slave trade. The slave trade was normal in the eighteenth century. As well as those who were directly involved, many others were indirectly involved, thinking nothing of investing in aspects of the trade, such as buying shares in ships and goods. People did not consider the feelings of those human beings whose lives were affected dreadfully by this industry. Wilberforce was a Member of Parliament and had distinguished himself by an extraordinary ability to communicate. He committed himself to the need to abolish this trade.

Based on today's attitudes anyone might think that Wilberforce was facing an easy task, but they would be very wrong. He faced incredible opposition from his peers, which only went to demonstrate the extent to which the slave trade was woven into the fabric of Britain at that time. Heartbreaking accounts, supported by other facts and figures, were not enough to convince people that this practice should stop. In fact it took Wilberforce many years of patient and committed work, in which he continued to respect the system and the individuals against whom he was fighting, as he sought to convince his peers that their mindset was wrong and that change was needed. It was not until 1807, 20 years after his first attempt, that the slave trade was at last abolished by Parliament. At last it was recognised that all people deserve to be respected, that all are equal.

The lesson we can learn from this is that it is important that we stick to our principles, and do not compromise them in order to fit in with those around us. Had Wilberforce not done this, the transatlantic slave trade would have continued and the lives of many would have been ruined and destroyed. Sadly, many lives continue to be wrecked by slavery, and we still need to stand up against it:

- 12.3 million people are victims of forced labour around the world (International Labour Organisation 2005).

- 1.2 million children (includes anyone under 18 years) are trafficked each year (UNICEF 2006).

- Human trafficking is one of the fastest growing organised crimes in the world (see www.unodc.org).

For more information on slavery today and on how you can get involved to make a difference, see the end of the session.

3.3 THE POINT OF THE CRIMINAL LAW

Group exercise 3.3: What's the point?

Instructions: Split into small groups. Use Question 1 to set the scene and then give the groups ten minutes to prepare an answer to Question 2. They should then be given no longer than two minutes to present their answer to the others, and following this a vote can be called to decide which group's ideas are the most popular.

Question 1: Imagine you are part of a community in which there are no laws. What do you imagine it would be like? Who would be the winners and losers?

NOTE

William Golding's novel *Lord of the Flies* sees a group of boys shipwrecked on an island. They initially recognise the need for government and set up a democratic system for making decisions. However, this is challenged as members of the community seek to step outside the 'laws'. As the relevance of these laws diminishes, so we get a glimpse of a community without laws. It is a place where force is king, where threats bring power, so that one person's views dictate all that happens, with the result that rules and 'law' are rejected in favour of 'breaking things up' (Golding 1954: 222). This lust for destruction seeks to eradicate any individuals who refuse to be dictated to – with tragic consequences.

Question 2: Your community believes that criminal laws might help deal with the growing problems within It, and has asked you to prepare a two-minute presentation stating what you believe the four most important laws should be. (Remember the discussions about safe and unsafe from the previous session.) This will be presented to others in the community, who will then vote on whose laws should be implemented. Be as creative as you like.

Discuss: It will be interesting to note what laws are chosen, as well as those that aren't. What areas of social life did the groups focus on, and why did they see these as particularly important? As you will see in the notes below, the criminal law developed as a means of protecting individuals and their property in a way that could be controlled. See if the groups mention similar ideas.

Even though we may sometimes think that life would be easier without laws, the criminal law stems from a desire to protect the peace, creating a society of order rather than chaos. Without laws, feuds would be common, the weak vulnerable, and justice hard to come by.

NOTES

The history of the criminal law provides many important lessons for us today. So it was, before there were criminal laws, individuals had to deal with 'wrongs' themselves. This meant that the individual became judge and jury, deciding who was guilty and what punishment they deserved. The result was that a mob would regularly see that 'justice' was delivered, although asking few questions along the way. Feuding was also common, as retaliations led to an over-reaction. By the state taking on the legislative role and identifying rules for all those who lived within its boundaries, more deliberation could be brought to the decision of who was guilty, and more consensus as to the type of punishment deserved. By involving the laws, feuding could be ended and justice be seen to be done. The result was a set of rules that aimed to allow mutual coexistence in which it was recognised what it was to live at 'peace'. A breach of this peace was seen as the perpetrator's breaking of his/her commitment to the community, thereby rejecting any rights to that peace; they therefore became outside the law – an 'outlaw'. (For more see Calhoun 1927; Cockburn 1977; Goebel 1976.)

Today, gun crime is a recurring story, which provides an example of what happens when people choose to live beyond the law. Gun crime (as discussed in Session 1, and which may link also to aspects of knife crime, discussed in Session 2) is about status and power; to achieve this individuals choose to live outside the law, applying a different moral code. If an individual gets 'wronged', then, rather than turning to the law of the land, they feel they must deal with it themselves in order to protect their 'power'. This response, however, leads to an over-reaction, which leaves the victim's group wanting revenge. Feuding begins in a search for justice, but it results only in an escalation of violence and more lives being ruined. Maybe today, if gangs engaged with the criminal law, these feuds could be ended, the spiral of revenge broken, and legitimate punishment brought to those who have done 'wrong'. This all raises the further question of why young people feel alienated by the law, for at its best the law seeks to provide them with a peaceful place to live, the same as everyone else. Discuss…

3.4. BREAK

3.5 SPOT THE CRIME

As we have seen, a crime is an action that is harmful to yourself or others. Another important element of a crime is the fact that the state has decided that anyone who is found guilty of committing that action should be punished, detailing this in a law. The criminal law covers many types of actions.

Shared exercise 3.5: Crimes

Instructions: Draw Table 3.5 on flipchart paper or on a whiteboard; see how many crimes the group can name in each section. Some examples of relevant crimes are listed for you in the table. Please note that this is far from an exhaustive list and the means of classification is crude, so don't spend too much time debating in which section the crimes should go. The exercise is only intended to get the group thinking about the range of the criminal law.

You may be able to name different laws, but can you spot them when they happen?

Table 3.5: Classifications of crimes

CRIMES AGAINST THE PERSON	PROPERTY CRIMES	VEHICLE CRIMES	ANTISOCIAL BEHAVIOUR
• assault/battery • assault occasioning ABH • assault occasioning GBH • obstructing a police officer • sexual offences (sexual assault, rape) • possession of drugs • intent to supply drugs • trafficking drugs • kidnap • murder	• theft • burglary • handling stolen goods • fraud • criminal damage • obtaining property by deception • abstracting electricity • going equipped • arson	• taking a vehicle without consent • interfering with a vehicle • driving without proper documentation • driving while intoxicated through drink or drugs • making off without payment • failure to stop/report an accident • trespass/throwing stones on railways	• causing harassment, alarm or distress • affray • riot • carrying offensive weapons • malicious communication • breach of antisocial behaviour orders • ticket touting

Group exercise 3.5: Spot the crime

Instructions: This exercise can be done by the groups in full, or in part, looking at particular questions you choose. Or the exercise could be run as a quiz, with you reading out the questions and the group as a whole coming up with answers that you can discuss straightaway.

Sheet 3.5a provides the questions, and Sheet 3.5b provides you with a set of answers. Please note that detailed answers have been provided to help with explanation and for interest, not to over-complicate the exercise.

DO EXERCISE.

Discuss: Using Sheet 3.5b, review the answers the groups have come up with, considering:

- the complex and varied nature of the law

- that ignorance of the law cannot be used as a defence

- that the law covers a wide range of behaviours.

The criminal law is varied and complex, covering a wide range of behaviours. You are expected to know what is and is not a crime from the age of 10 years in England and Wales; after that ignorance of the law is no defence. This is not always easy. It is, therefore, important to continue to think about our actions in relation to other people and the impact they will have on them.

SPOT THE CRIME: 'STAN'S BAD DAY' – QUESTIONS

Read the information *carefully* before answering the questions!
Make a note of the following:

- If an offence has been committed – what is it and who committed it?

- If an offence has not been committed – why?

Crimes against the person

1. Stan had just got up and is on his way to buy a newspaper, when he sees Anya and Ben on their way to school. They are in Year 12. As they pass Charlie (Year 9), Ben suggests they trip him up and film it on Anya's phone, as he thinks it would be funny. So while Ben trips Charlie and kicks him, Anya videos it.

   a) **Have any offences been committed?**

   b) **Anya then posts the video on 'Facebook' – is this an offence?**

2. Stan decides a bit of exercise will do him good before a busy day, so heads to the gym for a game of early morning five-a-side football. His mates Dave and Ed are playing. Ed wants the ball, so tackles Dave at speed. Ed gets the ball but knocks Dave's leg at the same time. Dave is seriously injured and his leg is fractured.

   Has Ed committed an offence?

Property crime

3. On leaving the gym, Stan overhears a conversation between Fiona (aged 9) and Gerry (aged 11). Fiona tells Gerry that last night she broke into a house and stole £1000 worth of items that included jewellery and electrical goods.

   a) Has Fiona committed an offence?

   Gerry truthfully says, 'That's nothing. Last night I broke into a house and stole £5000 worth of stuff – beat that.'

   b) Has Gerry committed an offence?

   Fiona asks Gerry if he will look after the stuff she has taken. Gerry agrees and Fiona hands it over.

   c) Have any offences been committed?

4. After a long day at work, Stan is waiting at the bus stop to get home. Next to him are two teenagers, Jack and Kelly, one dressed as a witch, the other as a wizard. Kelly says, 'Great costumes for the party; it gives us an excuse to bring these brooms so that we can use them to destroy that stupid picture of us that is hanging in the school hall.'

   Have any offences been committed?

Vehicle crime

5. While Stan is still in the bus stop, a moped zooms in. The driver darts in between two moving buses, causing one to slam on the brakes. The driver moves over to a group of girls, revving his engine before stopping.

    a) Have any offences been committed?

    The driver laughs when one of his friends asks, 'Isn't that your brother's bike?' The driver nods, 'But it is not a problem. What he doesn't know won't harm him.'

    b) Have any offences been committed?

    The driver gets off the bike and passes a helmet to a girl. He says, 'I got my provisional licence today and passed that bike test – I'll teach you how to ride in the supermarket car park – get on.' The girl gets on and they drive away.

    c) Have any offences been committed?

Antisocial behaviour/drugs

6. Stan has decided to meet his friends at a party. When leaving he picks up a coat he thinks is his, but it isn't. He does not look in the coat and does not know what is in it. On the way home the police stop him and find a large quantity of cocaine in his pocket.

    Has Stan committed an offence?

7. Stan makes his way home through the park. He starts talking with three lads: they are 15, 16 and 17 years old. They offer him a beer that they have just bought from the local off-licence.

    a) Have any offences been committed?

    To celebrate the 15-year-old's birthday they also buy some fireworks. They ask if Stan wants to help light them, but it is 11.30pm and Stan is feeling tired, so he walks on home. As he does, he sees and hears the fireworks flash in the sky.

    b) Have any offences been committed?

SPOT THE CRIME: 'STAN'S BAD DAY' – ANSWERS

Crimes against the person

1a) Ben is guilty of assault (which may be ABH) and so is Anya, even though Anya did not actually make contact with Charlie (see *The Times*, 15/2/08). Had anything been taken in the attack then this attack would have become robbery, which involves stealing with force.

1b) Yes. Sending a message or other material which is offensive or indecent via a network like Facebook is an offence. It is also an offence simply to use such a site to cause annoyance or anxiety to others.

2.   Even though Ed was responsible for the serious injury that Dave received, it was done within the rules of the game. When we play sports that involve physical contact we are consenting to any knocks that might arise within the game. Had Ed tackled Dave after the game had finished, he could be responsible for an assault causing GBH.

Property crime

3a) Fiona cannot be guilty of an offence, as she is under the age of criminal responsibility. On reaching the age of 10 years a child becomes fully criminally responsible, and they are then expected by the courts to know what is and is not a crime; ignorance is no defence.

3b) Gerry has committed a burglary by breaking into the house and then stealing from it.

3c) Getting involved in looking after, selling or hiding goods that you know are stolen falls within the offence of handling stolen goods.

4. Possessing articles (the brooms) for causing criminal damage (the actual legislation calls this offence 'having articles with intent to destroy or damage property'). Criminal damage takes place when someone destroys or damages someone else's property with no good reason. Even though the picture at the school is of them, it is not their property, and their intent to destroy it, even though they have not yet done it, means that they have committed the offence. This offence has wide application and also covers, for example, graffiti artists on their way to paint.

Vehicle crime

5a) Careless and inconsiderate driving is an offence that is caused when someone drives without proper consideration for those around them. The driver may also have committed an offence of causing harassment as a result of all the noise he is making. These offences also cover the use of vehicles off road.

5b) Taking the bike without proper consent of his brother is an offence. The driver would also need to have all the proper paperwork to drive this bike. For example, does he have insurance?

5c) It is an offence for the driver to take a passenger on his bike while he only holds a provisional licence. Also, it would be an offence for the girl to ride the bike if she had not first completed her CBT (compulsory basic training – a test that must be taken before anyone can ride a moped or motor vehicle in a public place).

Antisocial behaviour/drugs

6. To be found guilty of being in possession of a controlled drug, the individual must know that they had the drug in their possession; Stan did not know and therefore no offence has been committed.

Note: Drugs are classified into three different classes: A, B and C. Whatever class a drug falls in, it is still a criminal offence to be in possession of it. For more information about drugs see the websites at the end of this session.

7a) It is an offence for them to be sold alcohol, but there is no offence of being in possession of alcohol. The police do have a power to confiscate alcohol belonging to under-18s in public. If the person refuses to do what the police ask, then they commit an offence.

7b) All three are guilty of two offences. The first is being in possession of fireworks. You must be 18 years old or over if you want to have adult fireworks (covers most fireworks apart from items such as party poppers or sparklers) in a public place. They have also used these fireworks. It is an offence for them to be used between 11pm and 7am except on certain festivals.

Note: Concern over the way young people use alcohol stems not only from the health effects that result from binge drinking but also from the relationship between alcohol and violent crime. For the period 2005–06, 44 per cent (Office for National Statistics 2007) of all violent offences were committed by people under the influence of alcohol. This leaves the question, how many lives would have been better off, if those offenders had had a different attitude towards drinking?

NOTES

The criminal law has developed over many centuries and, as mentioned above, is highly complex. At street level the police will be interested in identifying whether an individual has committed the different elements of an offence. For example, with theft they will be considering whether the individual has:

a) dishonestly

b) appropriated (taken for their own)

c) property

d) belonging to another

e) with the intention of permanently depriving (of keeping the property and not returning it) someone else of it.

Each of these elements must be proved if someone is to be found guilty. Lawyers will then look at the offence with a further degree of scrutiny, considering whether each element is fully satisfied, and the strength of any defence. Even between England and Scotland there are differences between these legal definitions. Both the act itself and the mental attitude of the offender are considered.

Criminal responsibility: Before a child can be found guilty of a criminal offence, they must first reach an age of 'criminal responsibility'. This age is not fixed, and even in Europe there is much variation, ranging from 18 years in Luxembourg to 8 years in Scotland, which is the only European country where the age is lower than the 10 years in England, Wales and Northern Ireland. On reaching this age the young person is expected to have a good enough sense of what is right and wrong to know what is and is not a crime. As a result it becomes their responsibility to act within the law, facing punitive consequences should they break it (even though young people in Scotland are more likely to be dealt with by the children's hearing system, they can still be dealt with in adult courts if the offence is seen to be serious enough). However, in the context of promoting social participation, how appropriate is this expectation at a young age, particularly bearing in mind the complex nature of the law, differing individual moral codes, and the limited way in which these issues are addressed within education? Does the criminal law provide the best framework within which young people can develop their moral understanding, learning from their experiences and the mistakes that they make, or does it simply offer a means for the state to control young people from early in their lives, punishing them when they step out of line? (For more, see Muncie 2004.)

3.6 IMPACT OF CRIME ON THE OFFENDER

Often when we think of the impact of crime, we think about the victim. But remember being an offender also increases the likelihood of an individual becoming a victim of crime.

Exercise 3.6: Crime affects offenders

Instructions: You can just read out the accounts on Sheet 3.6, or you can hand the sheet out for the group to read themselves. Following this you can discuss the issues they raise.

Discuss: What is the group's response to these two examples, both of which are based on real life experiences? Reflect on the way in which crime damages relationships and limits opportunities. Remember, offenders are also the most likely group to be victims of crime.

CRIME AFFECTS OFFENDERS

Alex's story

I was 18 years old. I had been driving for just over a year. It had changed my life around. I had so many more opportunities. Thanks to being able to drive I got a new job and a serious girlfriend. She lived about 30 minutes away, but with the car it was no problem. It even improved my relationship with my mum and dad; it gave me this independence, which they really respected, and for the first time started to treat me more like an adult. And then one night, I don't know what I was thinking. I had only a couple of beers and was on my way to see my girlfriend. I didn't think it would be a problem, that was, until I took a corner too fast and crashed. No one was hurt and the car was hardly damaged, but the police turned up. They were really professional, even friendly; they asked me to blow into a breathalyser machine. I didn't think it would show positive but it did. They arrested me and took me back to the police station. I felt sick and nervous the whole way. There I had to be tested on a more sensitive machine and it too showed I was over the limit – I was a drunk driver. I phoned my mum; she was so upset when she heard that she walked out of the house and put my door keys down the drain. I got banned from driving. No car meant I lost my job; I also lost my girlfriend, not to mention the trust of my parents.

Gary's story

Didn't really enjoy school – but I was clever; teachers told me I could really achieve something. I might even have been the first one in my family to have gone to university – I guess my parents would have liked that. But friends and fun took over and so did my desire to spend money. Alcohol and cigarettes quickly led on to drugs, and once I started I found I just wanted more and more. I started to become obsessed about where my next fix was coming from, I could not concentrate at work and so lost my job and found myself spending each day seeing what I could steal so I could pay to fuel my habit. I got warned the first time I got caught shoplifting, but when it happened again and again I eventually ended up in prison. My family don't want to know me any more; every time I see my brother we argue. Last time was when I was sleeping on his floor after I came out of a drug rehabilitation centre. At least I'm known pretty well by the local police, but it would be better if I was remembered for something more than being yet another shoplifting junkie.

Discuss…

3.7 ENFORCING THE LAW

As we have seen, the purpose of the criminal law is to keep people safe, to keep people living in 'peace'. All societies have some set of rules or customs that governs behaviour.

Question 1: Whose responsibility is it to see criminal laws are enforced?

The point of this question is to encourage the group to reflect on the idea that there may well be those who are employed to 'police' the criminal law, but really the responsibility to implement it lies with us as individuals. The criminal law can only work effectively with the support of members of the community, which includes young and old.

Question 2: Is it important to have a group like the police to enforce the law? If so, why?

The police have particular powers, which allow them to react if a crime is committed. They are also part of the 'justice' system, which means that rather than leaving it for the individuals to respond to breaches of the law themselves, the police act on behalf of the state to ensure that the right procedures are followed, so that a fair and proper outcome can be reached. Police powers are a major focus in Session 4.

3.8 CONCLUSION

1. Review session

The criminal law marks for society what is seen as acceptable and unacceptable. At its best the criminal law provides a sense of order that allows everyone within that society to live in 'peace'. Those who break the laws step outside of the usual protection that the society offers and can be punished for what they have done. These laws apply equally to all members of the community on reaching an age of criminal responsibility. From that moment they are expected not only to abide by the law but to know what it says. The responsibility for enforcing the criminal law is everyone's, working together to create communities which are safe for all to live in.

Session outcomes should include participants:

○ considering effective communication and making a stand

○ recognising the point and purpose of the criminal law

○ understanding the range and complexity of the criminal law

○ recognising the impact of crime on an offender

○ realising the responsibility we all have to enforce the criminal law.

2. Reporting crime

The themes raised in the session encourage young people to recognise that they have a role in enforcing the law. Check that the group is aware of how they can do that; dialling 999 is not the only option. Crimestoppers (see web address below) provides a confidential way to report crimes.

3. Date of next session

Project ideas

1. Alcohol and young people's attitudes towards it are under constant scrutiny. Why not investigate this issue for yourselves? Find out more about other young people's attitudes towards alcohol, why they use it, and whether they understand the health implications connected with it.

2. Feuding is common among those who wish to stand outside of the criminal law. Develop your own campaign on questioning a culture of feuding and making sure that real justice is done.

3. Find out more about issues relating to drugs. Invite an expert in to talk to you on the subject. This might include a police officer or even an ex-offender.

4. If you come across an aspect of the law that you do not agree with or you think is missing, see if you can develop a constructive campaign to bring about change.

Helpful websites

- **www.antislavery.org** – information on slavery and the fight against it

- **www.crimestoppers-uk.org** – anonymous way to report any information about a crime – phone 0800 555 111

- **www.directgov.org.uk** – official UK Government website on the public services – information for new drivers/riders, as well as more on crimes and victims

- **www.howardleague.org** – the Howard League for Penal Reform – information about prisons and the consequences of crime

- **www.opsi.gov.uk/acts** – Office of Public Sector Information – see what is in an Act of Parliament

- **www.parliament.uk** – information about what takes place in the UK Houses of Parliament

- **www.release.org.uk** – Release – advice and information on drugs, the law and human rights

- **www.stopthetraffik.org** – information on human trafficking and ways to take a stand against it

- **www.talktofrank.com** – A–Z of drugs, their effects, and related legislation – including information on alcohol

- **www.unodc.org** – Crime Prevention Resources and Information – site of United Nations Office on Drugs and Crime; provides information about organised crime and trafficking

- **www.unicef.org.uk** – the UK committee for UNICEF – for facts about child trafficking

- **www.unlock.org.uk** – Unlock, the National Association of Reformed Offenders – information about the challenges facing ex-offenders

BIBLIOGRAPHY

References

Calhoun, G. (1927) *The Growth of Criminal Law in Ancient Greece.* Berkeley: University of California Press.

Cockburn, J. (ed.) (1977) *Crime in England 1550–1800.* London: Methuen.

Frankel, S. (2006) *Getting it Right: An Exploration of Children's Engagement with Morality within Their Everyday Lives.* PhD thesis, unpublished, Sheffield University Library.

Goebel, J. (1976) *Felony and Misdemeanour.* Pennsylvania: University of Pennsylvania Press.

Golding, W. (1954) *Lord of the Flies.* London: Faber and Faber.

International Labour Organisation (2005) *A Global Alliance Against Forced Labour.* Geneva: International Labour Office.

Muncie, J. (2004) *Youth Crime: A Critical Introduction.* London: Sage.

Office for National Statistics (2007) *Social Trends.* Basingstoke: Palgrave Macmillan.

Times, The (15/2/08) 'Girl faces jail for happy slap pictures'

UNICEF (2006) 'Information Sheet on Child Trafficking', accessed on 3/5/08, www.unicef.org.uk/publication/pub_detail.asp?pub_id=9

Further reading

Hague, W. (2007) *William Wilberforce: The Life of the Great Anti-Slave Trade Campaigner.* London: HarperCollins.

Metaxas, E. (2007) *Amazing Grace: William Wilberforce and the Heroic Campaign to End Slavery.* Oxford: Monarch.

Session 4

STREET LAW

SESSION OVERVIEW

The criminal law is a measure of what is and is not acceptable. In the last session we looked at what makes up a crime and why laws are important. Within this we looked briefly at whose role it is to enforce the law. As well as all of us having a duty to ensure that our communities provide conditions where everyone can live peacefully, there are certain groups that have particular powers. One of those is, of course, the police. This session looks at some of the common powers that the police use out on the streets. This will only be an overview, as going into too much detail would lead us into many more sessions. However, it is hoped that it will add to participants' understanding of issues around stop and search, arrest, and what happens on arriving at a police station. It will show that the proper use of these powers can be very different from what is seen on television, and will look to break down any misunderstandings that participants may have. Through raising awareness of police powers, it will also give young people a better understanding of their rights, empowering them further as citizens within their communities.

It is important for facilitators to be aware that the law is very complicated. Further guidance has been provided for facilitators to use as needed, but it is important not to get too caught up in the detail. Do be aware that the information in this session only provides a partial view of the law in this area, and that the law is also subject to change. Therefore, if participants have further questions or queries about ways that they have been treated, for example, they should be encouraged to seek legal advice. (See websites at the end of the session.)

Aims

- to raise awareness of everyday powers used by the police

- to explain the basics of stop and search powers under the Police and Criminal Evidence Act 1984 (PACE) and what they are for

- to raise awareness of the police power of arrest

- to raise awareness of the process after arrest – being taken to a police station

- to build on practical skills looked at in previous sessions.

Session 4 timed outline

ACTION	TIME IN MINUTES	DESCRIPTION	RESOURCES	NOTES
1. Introduction	5	• welcome • refresh ground rules • re-cap Session 3 • introduce Session 4	Flipchart	
2. Antisocial behaviour	10	There is a great focus on antisocial behaviour. Question: What is antisocial behaviour? In groups: Consider actions of Sheet 4.2; put into order of what is most commonly seen as antisocial. Discuss the suggestion that hanging around with friends is seen as antisocial behaviour. Antisocial behaviour is an action that causes upset or fear to others. (Legal definition is cause harassment, alarm or distress.)	4.2	
3. Stop and search (1)	25	Police have special powers to investigate and prevent crime. Question: What are your experiences of the police and stop and search? Stop and search is controversial and raises strong emotions. In groups: 1. prepare arguments using Sheets 4.3a and 4.3b 2. debate the suggestion that 'more stop and search is a good idea to prevent youth crime'. Stop and search can be useful but it must be used in a respectful and responsible way.	4.3a 4.3b	
4. Break	5			

Session 4 timed outline continued

5. Stop and search (2)	15	The police have different powers to stop and search, the main power comes under PACE. To make a stop the police must follow certain steps. In groups: 1. Together go through Sheet 4.5a, using the Facilitator's Guide, Sheet 4.5b, for more information. 2. Ask groups to answer questions on Sheet 4.4. 3. Go through answers – Sheet 4.5c.	4.5a 4.5b 4.5c
6. Arrest	10	Arrests are very different to what we see on TV. Shared exercise: 1. Together go through criteria of arrest, Sheet 4.6a, using guidance notes as needed. 2. Act out scenario – see Sheet 4.6a 3. Discuss what happened to Kofi, using answers on Sheet 4.6b.	4.6a 4.6b
7. Arriving at a police station	15	After an arrest the detained person must be taken straight to a police station. In groups: 1. Go through rights at the police station (Sheet 4.6a) using guidance notes – Sheet 4.7a. 2. Look at custody record exercise – Sheet 4.7b. 3. Go through answers.	4.6a 4.7a 4.7b
8. Conclusion	5	1. Review session. Through knowledge of the law participants should be more aware of what the police have to do and why, as well as having greater awareness of what their own rights are. 2. Check everyone is okay. 3. Date of next session.	

Outcomes

Session outcomes will include participants:

- having a better understanding of what antisocial behaviour is

- having a greater awareness of police powers out on the streets

- developing further their ability to make an argument and to use listening skills

- furthering their knowledge of the law and their rights and responsibilities as citizens

- being empowered to participate more fully within society, through increased knowledge

- recognising what the police have to do and why, as part of working to make communities safer.

4.1 INTRODUCTION TO SESSION 4

Welcome

1. Welcome group to the session.

2. Refresh your ground rules.

3. Re-cap themes from Session 3.

a) Remind the group that some of the issues you addressed in Session 3 included:

    ○ considering effective communication and making a stand

    ○ recognising the point and purpose of the criminal law

    ○ understanding the range and complexity of the criminal law

    ○ recognising the impact of crime on an offender

    ○ realising the responsibility we all have to enforce the criminal law.

b) Ask if anyone has had any thoughts on the issues raised since the last session.

Introduce Session 4

To be a citizen it is important that, as well as realising our responsibilities, which we have looked at in detail over the last few sessions, that we are also aware of our rights. As we have seen in Session 3, Parliament passes laws to define what is and is not acceptable in society. We all have a duty to enforce these laws, but certain groups are given particular powers to do this. This session will look at some of the powers the police have and how they can be used. It will look particularly at issues around stop and search, arrest, and what happens after an arrest when someone arrives at the police station. If you come into contact with the police, the information in this session will help you to understand better what the police can do as part of their job, but also what they have to do, in order to respect your rights as citizens. An outline of this session is as follows:

1. Introduction to Session 4
2. Antisocial behaviour
3. Stop and search (1)
4. Break
5. Stop and search (2)
6. Arrest
7. Arriving at a police station
8. Conclusion to Session 4.

4.2 ANTISOCIAL BEHAVIOUR

This session is all about looking at police powers out on the streets. Over the last few years the police have been asked to focus more and more on behaviour that is seen to be antisocial. It is becoming a common reason for young people to find themselves in contact with the police.

Group exercise 4.2: What is antisocial behaviour?

Instructions: Split into groups. Get some general thoughts by asking the question below, before having a go at the exercise. Cut out the statements on Sheet 4.2, a set for each group. Ask the groups to put the statements in order, from what they see as the biggest antisocial 'problem' to the least.

General question: What is antisocial behaviour?

DO EXERCISE.

Answer: These figures are based on respondents being asked what, out of the seven areas of behaviour below, they perceived as being the biggest problem.

- young people hanging around on the streets   33 per cent
- leaving rubbish   31 per cent
- vandalism, graffiti and other deliberate damage to property   28 per cent
- people using or dealing drugs   28 per cent
- people being drunk or rowdy in a public place   26 per cent
- noisy neighbours   11 per cent
- abandoned and burnt-out cars   9 per cent

(Home Office 2007: 103)

Discuss: What is the group's reaction to this? Is it right that young people just hanging around should be seen as the greatest antisocial problem (a perception that has been increasing over recent years)? How does this fit with earlier themes, for example 'mutual respect' and 'breaking down barriers'?

It can be really hard to define what antisocial behaviour is, as different people have different views, but it is generally actions that cause upset or fear to others. It certainly provides a common area of contact, even conflict, between young people and the police and other members of the public. Even after asking yourself whether 'this' action makes you and others feel safe or not (Session 3), you may still find some people who see the act as unacceptable, as antisocial. Remember, if you act with respect towards such people, then there is going to be a greater chance of breaking down barriers and helping them to see beyond the stereotypes they hold (see themes from Session 1). However, this might take time and involve you listening to their concerns and reacting to them.

NOTES: ANTISOCIAL BEHAVIOUR – WHAT DO YOU THINK?

Antisocial behaviour is a very common story in the press and a constant theme on politicians' agendas. This focus on antisocial behaviour provides a good example of how stereotypes of young people as a threat have resulted in adults focusing on ways of controlling that threat through more legislation, rather than perhaps looking to find ways of really dealing with the underlying issues. For example, if the problem is young people hanging out on the streets, then, rather than increasing police powers to disperse groups[1] or using devices called Mosquitoes (a piece of equipment that emits a buzzing sound) to prevent young people congregating in certain areas, consider what provision is made in neighbourhoods to create suitable space for young people to hang out, to spend time with their friends. The way we think about and deal with antisocial behaviour goes to the heart of building communities based on mutual respect. For if young people are to be encouraged to take on their role as citizens, it is important that adults recognise that they also have rights, and proper provision needs to be made so that they can live their lives. It would be wrong to suggest that in some areas and with some young people antisocial behaviour is not a problem, but should that impact on *all* young people?

---

1   Where two or more young people have or are likely to cause harassment, alarm or distress, the police have the power to require the group to disperse. Police have similar powers throughout the UK.

WHAT IS ANTISOCIAL BEHAVIOUR?

Young people hanging around on the streets	**Leaving rubbish**
Vandalism, graffiti and other deliberate damage to property	**People using or dealing drugs**
People being drunk or rowdy in a public place	**Abandoned and burnt-out cars**
Noisy neighbours	

4.3 STOP AND SEARCH (1)

In order to deal with antisocial behaviour and with crime more generally, the police have been granted special powers by Parliament. These powers allow them to investigate crimes even before they happen. One of the powers the police use most frequently on the streets is stop and search.

Shared exercise 4.3: Stop and search

Question 1: What are your experiences of the police?

Question 2: What, if any, are your experiences of being stopped and searched?

Record any thoughts on a flipchart, as these may be useful in the following exercise.

Group exercise 4.3: 'More stop and search is a good idea in preventing youth crime!'

Stop and search is used to make communities safer places but it is a controversial power and continues to raise strong emotions. It also results in an encounter that can shape the way young people come to think about the police. It is therefore important that it is used in a respectful and responsible way. You are going to look at some arguments around stop and search.

Instructions: This exercise builds on listening skills and effective communication, looked at in previous sessions.

Split the group into two/four groups depending on numbers; one half to argue for, the other against, the following motion:

> 'We believe more stop and search is a good idea
> to prevent youth crime.'

Sheets 4.3a and 4.3b have been designed to help participants in shaping their arguments. Note that they contain identical facts but different quotes. Participants may also wish to refer to personal responses from the group that came up in looking at the questions above.

Give groups time to prepare their arguments. Choose two groups to debate with each other, two minutes each to state their case and then one minute each to reply, followed by questions from the floor and a quick 30 seconds of summing up from each side (alter timings as necessary). It may be helpful to ring a bell 10 seconds before they reach the time limit, warning them to bring their thoughts to a close. Those teams not directly involved in arguing for or against should be tasked with preparing questions to ask the two teams, as well as taking on the role of adjudicator: spot the common ground; who argued their case best?

DO EXERCISE.

An ideal conclusion: Stop and search can be useful. However, it also has the power to damage relationships and therefore needs to be used carefully. It is important that those being stopped and those who are doing the stopping strive to treat each other with mutual respect, recognising that both parties want to ensure a safe community.

4.4 BREAK

'MORE STOP AND SEARCH IS A GOOD IDEA IN PREVENTING YOUTH CRIME!' (1)

Some facts:

• Police can investigate a suspicion of a crime without having to arrest someone. • Investigation can take place on streets causing only short inconvenience to innocent parties. • Having the capacity to do a quick check into a set of factors that create suspicion has the potential to allow police to focus their work and time more effectively.	• Stop and search has the potential to damage relationships with the community and therefore its use must be respectful and responsible • Getting stop and search wrong only creates barriers to the police's ability to do their job, and stops members of the community getting access to the services they deserve.

In 2006:

- police stopped 888,700 people and/or vehicles, 3 per cent more than 2004/5

- 12 per cent of searches led to an arrest. (Ministry of Justice 2007a)

Reasons for searches 2005/6 (Ministry of Justice 2007a)							
Drugs	Stolen property	Going equipped*	Offensive weapons	Criminal damage	Firearms	Other**	TOTAL
377,900	204,600	102,800	77,500	28,100	13,300	74,200	888,700

*Having items with you to commit theft-related offences. **Includes public order and prevention of terrorism powers.

- Of those stopped and searched:
  - 75 per cent are white
  - 15 per cent are black
  - 8 per cent are Asian
  - 2 per cent are ethnic origin.

- As a proportion of the population:
  - black people are seven times more likely to get searched than white people
  - Asian people are twice as likely to get searched as white people.

- Drugs are the most common reason for black and Asian people to be stopped and searched. (Ministry of Justice 2007b)

Ken Jones, ACPO (Association of Chief Police Officers) President, said: 'Used fairly, stop and search has proven to be a powerful tool for tackling and preventing crime to the benefit of all. We need to look at using these powers more efficiently in ways that don't undermine community confidence in policing'. (ACPO 2008)

John Dunford, the General Secretary of the Association of School and College Leaders, said [about new powers in schools that] additional search powers would be welcome. 'This sends a strong message that heads will not tolerate students using alcohol and drugs and that they have the power to deal swiftly with students who break the rules.' (*The Guardian*, 27/3/08)

A 16-year-old from Hackney…thinks greater protection makes the hassle of being searched repeatedly worthwhile. 'People are carrying blades and guns. They're looking for trouble. This will make things safer,' he reasons. 'I don't have anything to worry about because I don't carry weapons.' (*BBC News*, 31/1/08)

'If the police cannot be trusted to conduct stop and search on a fair basis, the public will soon find out… But as a black man, who has been searched and is very likely to be stopped under these new rules, I believe they will make the streets safer for us all.' (Shaun Bailey, *The Sunday Times*, 3/2/08)

'MORE STOP AND SEARCH IS A GOOD IDEA IN PREVENTING YOUTH CRIME!' (2)

Some facts:

• Police can investigate a suspicion of a crime without having to arrest someone. • Investigation can take place on streets causing only short inconvenience to innocent parties. • Having the capacity to do a quick check into a set of factors that create suspicion has the potential to allow police to focus their work and time more effectively.	• Stop and search has the potential to damage relationships with the community and therefore its use must be respectful and responsible. • Getting stop and search wrong only creates barriers to the police's ability to do their job, and stops members of the community getting access to the services they deserve.

In 2006:

- police stopped 888,700 people and/or vehicles, 3 per cent more than 2004/5

- 12 per cent of searches led to an arrest. (Ministry of Justice 2007a)

Reason for searches 2005/6 (Ministry of Justice 2007a)

Drugs	Stolen property	Going equipped*	Offensive weapons	Criminal damage	Firearms	Other**	TOTAL
377,900	204,600	102,800	77,500	28,100	13,300	74,200	888,700

*Having items with you to commit theft-related offences. **Includes public order and prevention of terrorism powers.

- Of those stopped and searched:
  - 75 per cent are white
  - 15 per cent are black
  - 8 per cent are Asian
  - 2 per cent are ethnic origin.

- As a proportion of the population:
  - black people are seven times more likely to get searched than white people
  - Asian people are twice as likely to get searched as white people.

- Drugs are the most common reason for black and Asian people to be stopped and searched. (Ministry of Justice 2007b)

Karen Chouhan, a trustee of the 1990 Trust, emphasizes the following: 'The murder of young people through the easy availability of guns and knives is completely unacceptable and every life lost is one too many. The 1990 Trust works directly with victims of these crimes – mothers and relatives of the deceased. The solution must be a carefully considered one and must be backed by a proportionate amount of resources determined by the enormity and complexity of the cycle of violence. An intensified stop and search targeted at black communities is set to backfire with serious ramifications for community relations and policing.' Karen adds that 'available statistics of stop-and-search do not make a compellingly convincing argument for an escalated use of stop-and-search'. (Blink 2007)

Hundreds of airport-style metal detectors are to be deployed by police on Britain's streets under aggressive plans by government to combat soaring knife crime… Shami Chakrabarti, director of the human rights group Liberty, warned that 'electronic stop and search' could have an 'incendiary' effect on community relations, unless handled sensitively. She said it could create further tensions if mishandled by police on crowded inner city streets. (*The Sunday Times*, 17/2/08)

An 18-year-old student, decked in the latest sportswear, says he already gets stopped 'at least three times a week' and isn't keen on the idea of becoming more intimately acquainted with police officers. 'Whenever it happens it makes me angry and I hate them. This'll just make things worse,' he says. 'One time I was with my girl when they stopped me,' he recalls. 'They told me a robbery happened way down the road, and I just thought "What's that got to do with me? It was embarrassing in front of her." (*BBC News*, 31/1/08)

4.5 STOP AND SEARCH (2)

The police have different powers of stop and search. But the most common comes under legislation called the Police and Criminal Evidence Act 1984; it is known as PACE for short. PACE allows a police officer to stop and search someone in a public place, without them being under arrest. But there are certain steps that the officer must follow. The handout provides a basic guide to some of the key issues the officer must consider.

Group exercise 4.5: Spot the stop

Instructions

1. Go through Sheet 4.5a, 'Spot the stop – Key law 1', with groups, making use of the additional facilitator's guide: Sheet 4.5b, 'Stop and search'.

2. Ask the group to use the information on the handout to answer the scenario questions.

3. Answer questions. See Sheet 4.5c, 'Spot the stop – Facilitator's answer sheet'.

Stop and search depends on what someone sees as reasonable suspicion. This can cause conflict and be difficult to challenge. Therefore, if people do find themselves being stopped and searched, it is going to be a much easier experience to work with the police rather than against them. However, using the knowledge gained above, young people can make sure their rights are respected, and if they do have an issue then this can be addressed at a later stage.

NOTES: POLICE COMMUNITY SUPPORT OFFICERS

Police Community Support Officers (PCSOs) are increasingly being used to provide the police with an additional presence in communities. The PCSOs are not police officers and do not have the same powers. However, they do have certain powers that can impact on young people. These include (not a complete list):

- giving fixed penalty notices for antisocial behaviour or littering

- requiring a person to give their name and address for offences such as:

  - acting in an antisocial way

  - causing injury or distress to someone

  - causing loss or damage to someone's property

- dispersing groups and taking anyone under 16 years home

- confiscating alcohol and tobacco and controlled drugs

- searching for alcohol or tobacco.

If someone makes off or does not comply with a PCSO, then they can detain them using reasonable force until a constable arrives.

Sheet 4.5a

SPOT THE STOP – KEY LAW 1

The officer must have **reasonable grounds** to **suspect** they will find **stolen or prohibited articles**.

This could include bladed articles or anything that might be used for criminal damage.

Test for reasonable suspicion:
Would a reasonable person (an average man or lady) be suspicious?

Suspicion **cannot be based on personal factors**, such as: age, skin colour and appearance.

The search

Officer must inform person **that they are detained** for the purpose of a search before explaining:

Grounds – what power they have to search

Object – what they are looking for

Warrant – must show warrant card if not in uniform

Identify – must identify themselves

Station – must say what station they are from

Entitlement – you can have a record of the search.

On the streets the detained person **must not** be asked **to remove** more than:

Jumper

Outer garments

Gloves.

'Stop and search must be used **fairly, responsibly, with respect** for people being searched and without unlawful discrimination.' (PACE Codes of Practice, 1.1)

Scenario 1:

a. It is 1am in an area that has had a problem with criminal damage. Two 17-year-old lads wearing hoodies are walking home. Do the officers have the power to stop them based on what they are wearing?

b. Would it make a difference if the officers had just received a radio call saying two men had been seen tagging a bus stop nearby?

Scenario 2:

a. Two male officers see two teenage girls carrying an empty box of fireworks. Do the officers have the power to stop the girls and ask them to explain this?

b. The girls say they don't know anything about the fireworks. Do the officers have the power to search the girls?

c. Can they ask them to take off the jackets that they are wearing?

Scenario 3:

a. A Police Community Support Officer stops a group of young people drinking alcohol; he suspects that they are carrying knives. Can the PCSO search them?

b. If, after seizing the alcohol the young people are drinking, the PCSO believes that a couple of the young people are hiding more alcohol on them, can the PCSO search them?

FACILITATOR'S GUIDE: STOP AND SEARCH

'Stop and search' under Section 1 of the Police and Criminal Evidence Act 1984 says:

Making the stop

1. To stop and search, the police must have reasonable grounds to suspect they will find stolen or prohibited articles. These include bladed articles or anything that might be used for criminal damage, burglary or theft, as well as fireworks or drugs.

2. The test for reasonable suspicion is: would a reasonable person be suspicious?

   Note: An officer can still suspect even if they are uncertain.

3. Suspicion can never be based just on personal factors such as age, skin colour and appearance.

   Note: Appearance can form reasonable suspicion in the case of gangs or groups who are distinctive by what they wear and are known to carry prohibited articles.

The search

4. Officers must inform an individual that they are being detained for the purpose of a search before explaining:

   Grounds – right to do search/what power they have

   Object – the purpose of the search/what they are looking for

Warrant – must show warrant card if not in uniform

Identify – must identify themselves

Station – must say what station they are from

Entitlement – must inform the person stopped they have a right to a record of the search.

5. While on the streets the detained person must not be asked to remove more than:

Jumper

Outer garments

Gloves

Note: This does not stop officers from putting hands in outer pockets as well as feeling around in socks, shoes or collar, if that is necessary. Officers can require other items of clothing to be removed, such as headgear or footwear, using different powers; if more clothing needs to be removed this must be done at a police station or out of public view, by an officer of the same sex.

6. Powers to 'stop and search must be used fairly, responsibly, with respect for people being searched and without unlawful discrimination' (PACE Codes of Practice, 1.1).

Note: This is a simplified version of the law. The police do have additional powers of stop and search that exceed the powers outlined above, in certain circumstances even taking away the need for reasonable suspicion. For example, a senior officer can give authorisation for anyone in a particular area to be searched if it is believed that an incident involving serious violence might take place or that people are carrying weapons. The officer on the streets needs no grounds to actually carry out the search. The police also have more broad powers to search after an arrest has been made.

For more guidance on stop and search see www.stopandsearch.com.

SPOT THE STOP – FACILITATOR'S ANSWER SHEET

Scenario 1

a. It is 1am in an area that has had a problem with criminal damage. Two 17-year-old lads wearing hoodies are walking home. Do the officers have the power to stop them based on what they are wearing?

No. The police need reasonable suspicion. What they are wearing does not provide the grounds for the search.

b. Would it make a difference if the officers had just received a radio call saying two men had been seen tagging a bus stop nearby?

Yes. This information could provide the reasonable suspicion that the police need.

Scenario 2

a. Two male officers see two teenage girls carrying an empty box of fireworks. Do the officers have the power to stop the girls and ask them to explain this?

Yes. The officers can stop someone and just ask them to account for themselves, as long as they have reasonable suspicion. However, note that the police have no power to stop someone in order to find grounds for a search.

b. The girls say they don't know anything about the fireworks. Do the officers have the power to search the girls?

Yes. The empty box of fireworks and their reaction is enough to form reasonable suspicion that the girls may have 'prohibited items' on them. As a result the officers would have a power to search.

c.   Can they ask them to take off the jackets that they are wearing?

Yes, although best practice may suggest that an officer of the same sex should carry out any search. Any further search must be carried out in private by officers of the same sex as the detained person.

Scenario 3

a.   A Police Community Support Officer stops a group of young people drinking alcohol; he suspects that they are carrying knives. Can the PCSO search them?

No. The PCSO has no power to stop and search under PACE, although in certain circumstances and with a police constable the PCSO can search.

b.   If, after seizing the alcohol the young people are drinking, the PCSO believes that a couple of the young people are hiding more alcohol on them, can the PCSO search them?

Yes. The PCSO has a particular power to search if the PCSO in trying to seize the alcohol reasonably believes that there is still alcohol in that person's possession. A PCSO cannot ask them to remove jumper, outer garments or gloves.

4.6 ARREST

Shared exercise 4.6: Arrest

You will have seen arrests in television programmes and in films, but these arrests would very rarely be seen as lawful by the courts. An arrest results in a person losing their liberty and their right to do what they please. In order for someone to lose this human right, certain criteria need to be met.

Opening question: What do the police need to do in order to arrest someone?

Instructions

1. Go through 'Arrest and arriving at a police station – Key law 2' (Sheet 4.6a) with participants, leaving out the information 'At the police station'. Make use of 'Key law – Notes for facilitators: Arrest'. (See next page.)

2. With this information in mind, ask the group to watch or read through the drama on their handout (Sheet 4.6a). This certainly works best if two of the participants or facilitators act out the encounter. Ask the others to spot what was done well and what was done badly.

3. Using Sheet 4.6b, work through questions and answers. You might want to have written the questions on a flipchart beforehand.

KEY LAW – NOTES FOR FACILITATORS: ARREST

The police have wide-ranging powers of arrest but generally they should only arrest someone if:

- the officer has reasonable suspicion that an offence will be, is being or has been committed

- they think there are reasonable grounds to believe (this is a legal term for a level of thought higher than suspicion) that the arrest is really necessary.

    Note: Could the situation be dealt with in another way – for example, by using a fixed penalty notice, thereby avoiding the need to arrest and take the person to the police station?

The officer must:

- take reasonable steps to inform a person that they are under arrest, which might be as little as saying 'You're "nicked"'

- state the legal power for the arrest and the factual grounds for it – the reason why they are making the arrest

- give the caution as soon as possible:

    a) You do not have to say anything,

    b) but it may harm your defence if you do not mention when questioned something which you later rely on in court.

    c) Anything you do say may be given in evidence.

The police can use reasonable force.

ARREST AND ARRIVING AT A POLICE STATION – KEY LAW 2

Arrest requires:
Reasonable suspicion
that **an offence**
has been committed, is being committed
or
will be committed
and
reasonable grounds to believe
that it is
necessary
to make that arrest.

The police can use reasonable force!

On arrest a person must be told:
• they are under arrest
• reason for the arrest
• the caution – as soon as possible…

1. You do not have to say anything…
2. but it may harm your defence if you do not mention when questioned something which you later rely on in court.
3. Anything you do say may be given in evidence.

Making an arrest – Drama

Officer: Excuse me, mate, what are you doing hanging around here?

Kofi: Nothing much, just waiting for a friend.

Officer: You know this is a place where people sell drugs? Don't you?

Kofi: No.

Officer: So have you got any drugs on you?

Kofi: No.

Officer: Take your coat off and give it here and then I can check it.

Kofi: Why should I?

Officer: Because I say so. Now pass it here and if you've got no drugs then you can be on your way. (Kofi starts to take jacket off.) Look, I haven't got time to mess around, let's deal with this at the station. You're nicked. You're wasting my time. Now anything you say can be used against you. Do you understand?

Kofi: This is crazy, I am just waiting for a lift home.

Officer: You can tell me all about it at the station, come on. (Officer takes hold of Kofi's arm and leads him off.)

At the police station

After taking the person under arrest straight to a police station, the custody sergeant who is responsible for a detained person must tell them of their rights:

1. to inform someone of their arrest

2. to get legal advice (if they want it)

3. to see the Codes of Practice

4. to have an appropriate adult present if they are under 17 years of age.

DO:

- inform someone of your arrest

- if you want legal advice, get it

- sign for property

- ask for a doctor if needed

- give correct details. (Otherwise you may cause problems with getting bail.)

DO NOT

until you have received legal advice (if you want it):

- sign the officer's notebook

- answer any questions about the offence. (You should not be questioned until you are given a proper interview.)

MAKING AN ARREST – FACILITATOR'S NOTES

Making an arrest – Drama

Officer:	Excuse me, mate, what are you doing hanging around here?
Kofi:	Nothing much, just waiting for a friend.
Officer:	You know this is a place where people sell drugs? Don't you?
Kofi:	No.
Officer:	So have you got any drugs on you?
Kofi:	No.
Officer:	Take your coat off and give it here and then I can check it.
Kofi:	Why should I?
Officer:	Because I say so. Now pass it here and if you've got no drugs then you can be on your way. (Kofi starts to take jacket off.) Look, I haven't got time to mess around, let's deal with this at the station. You're nicked. You're wasting my time. Now anything you say can be used against you. Do you understand?
Kofi:	This is crazy, I am just waiting for a lift home.
Officer:	You can tell me all about it at the station, come on. (Officer takes hold of Kofi's arm and leads him off.)

---

1. **Is there reasonable suspicion for an arrest?**

   No. Kofi simply being in an area known for drug dealing is not enough to create reasonable suspicion of an offence unless it is linked to other factors, such as the way Kofi is acting or items found on him after a search. His reluctance at first to agree to the search seems natural, as the officer has not explained his powers of reasons for asking him to take off his coat.

2. **Is arrest necessary?**

   No. There is no indication at the moment that this arrest is necessary. The officer could conduct a proper search out on the street, rather than wasting time by arresting Kofi and taking him to the police station.

3. **Is Kofi told he is under arrest?**

   Yes. Kofi is told he is being taken to the police station and that he is 'nicked'.

4. **Is Kofi told the reason for the arrest?**

   No. A reason is given but this is not a reason recognised by law. None of the proper factual or legal grounds are explained to Kofi.

5. **Cautioned?**

   No. Part of the caution is given but this is not good enough. There is no reason why the full caution could not have been given here and now.

4.7 ARRIVING AT A POLICE STATION

Group exercise 4.7: Arriving at a police station

After being arrested an individual should be taken straight to a police station that is able to hold suspects. Here, the suspect will be booked in by a custody sergeant who is responsible for their welfare while they are there. The custody sergeant is not part of the investigation into their case. While at the police station, an individual has certain rights.

Instructions: This exercise allows you together to consider an individual's rights at the police station. This is followed by an exercise for the participants to do in groups, looking at a custody record.

1. Go through the final section of Sheet 4.6a ('Arrest and arriving at a police station'), using the notes on Sheet 4.7a.

2. Split into groups and hand out Sheet 4.7b ('Hertenford Police – Custody record', model of blank record taken from Holtam 2001).

3. Explain as follows:

Having gone through the key law with the group, inform them now that they are the Superintendent of Langley Police Station. Kofi, who was arrested earlier, has now been booked in. The Superintendent has seen a CCTV recording of the arrest, and is reviewing the custody record. Is there anything that should concern him?

DO EXERCISE.

Concerns

1. The reason Kofi was given for his arrest on the street is very different from the one recorded at the station.

2. After arrest on the street Kofi did make a comment that has not been recorded.

3. There is a very long gap between the arrest and arriving at the police station.

4. The grounds for detention reflect further differences as to what happened out on the street, and the information (or lack of it) that Kofi was given on arrest.

5. Kofi is under 17 years of age and therefore should have an appropriate adult present.

6. The officer should not have signed the 'legal advice declined' section. Also, Kofi has not signed to say he does not want to inform someone of his arrest.

7. Has Kofi's ethnic origin been a factor in his wrongful search and arrest?

ARRIVING AT THE POLICE STATION – FACILITATOR'S NOTES

1. Arrested person must be taken without delay to a designated police station.

NOTE: A designated police station is one that is equipped to hold people in custody, until they are released by the police (as they are not continuing with the matter or on bail; being required to return to the police station at a later date) or held there until taken to court.

2. A custody sergeant, who is independent of the investigation, is responsible for the individual while in custody.

NOTE: Anyone who has been arrested is taken to a custody suite, where a sergeant who is independent of the investigation is in charge of their welfare. While in custody a person has certain legal rights as well as rights to food, water and medical care.

3. A detained person has the right to:

   a) inform someone of their arrest

   b) legal advice

   c) see the Codes of Practice.

NOTE: In most cases individuals at the police station have the right to tell someone they have been arrested: a phone call to a member of the family or friend. They have the right to legal advice, which is free, and, even if someone does not have their own solicitor, there will be a duty solicitor who will be able to help. It is the role of the solicitor to advise the individual about their legal rights while at the police station, supporting them through the police interview. The detained person can also look at the Codes of Practice, a guidance book, which outlines best practice.

4. The person detained is not to be asked about the offence on the way to the police station or, when arrived, until a proper interview is given.

5. An appropriate adult is required to support anyone under 17 years of age.

NOTE: An appropriate adult should also support anyone under 17 years of age. An appropriate adult might be the young person's parent or guardian, a social worker or some other suitable adult over 18 years of age. The role of the appropriate adult is to support the young person and to ensure that they fully understand what is going on around them.

DO:

- inform someone of arrest
- if legal advice is wanted, get it
- sign for property
- ask for a doctor if needed
- give correct details (otherwise might cause problems with getting bail).

DO NOT:

until legal advice is received (if wanted):

- sign the officer's notebook
- answer any questions about offence (should not be questioned until a proper interview is given).

Sheet 4.7b

HERTENFORD POLICE – CUSTODY RECORD

| Station: LANGLEY | EM No: | Custody Number | NW | 435 | 2 |

1. Reasons for Arrest: ARRESTED ON SUSPICION OF CAUSING CRIMINAL DAMAGE

2. Comment made by person if present when the facts of arrest explained
Yes [ ] No [✓] If yes record on Log of Events

3. Place of Arrest CAR PARK : LANGLEY HIGH STREET

4.

	Time	Date
Arrested at:	13:40	1/4/08
Arrived at Station:	14:40	1/4/08
Relevant Time:	14:40	1/4/08

Condition on Arrival: UPSET

Relevant time not applicable [ ] tick if appropriate

5. DETENTION DECISION *Delete as appropriate

A. Detention authorised*
B. Detention not authorised*

Signature: Jacks
Name: LIN JACKS
Time: 14:45   Date: 1/4/08

REASON FOR DETENTION

(i) To charge: [ ]
&/or (ii) Other authority: [ ]
&/or (iii) Other secure or preserve evidence: [ ]
&/or (iv) To obtain evidence by questioning: [✓]

Record grounds for detention
ON SEARCH KEYS FOUND BELIEVED TO HAVE BEEN USED FOR SCRATCHING CARS IN LOCAL AREA. ARRESTED DETAINED FOR QUESTIONING

Person present when grounds read: [✓]
Person informed of grounds: [ ]

6. Comment made by person when informed of detention
Yes [ ] No [✓]
If yes record on Log of Events

7. Drugs referral information leaflet issued: N/A
Time: .... Date: ....

OFFICER OPENING CUSTODY RECORD
Signature: Jacks
Name: LIN JACKS   Rank: SGT
Time: 14:45   Date: 1/4/08

8. PERSONAL DETAILS
Surname: MULLWAH
Forename(s): KOFI
Address: 36a, THE VILLAS LANGLEY
Telephone number: 813 245
Occupation: STUDENT
Age: 16   Date of birth: 25/7/91
Height: 155   Sex: (male) female
Ethnic origin: BLACK
Place of birth: LONDON

9. Arresting Officer: JOHN RANDALL
Rank: PC   No: 521   Station: LANGLEY

10. Officer in the case: JOHN RANDALL
Rank: PC   No: 521   Station: LANGLEY

11. DETAINED PERSONS RIGHTS
An extract from a notice setting out my rights has been read to me and I have been given a copy. I have also been provided with a written setting out my entitlements while in custody. SIGNATURE: Kofi Mullwah
Time: 14:50   Date: 1/4/08

LEGAL ADVICE REQUESTED
I want to speak to a solicitor as soon as practicable:
Signature: ....
Time: ....   Date: ....

LEGAL ADVICE DECLINED
I have been informed that I may speak to a solicitor IN PERSON or ON THE TELEPHONE:
Signature: John Randall
Time: 15:00   Date: 1/4/08
I DO NOT WANT TO SPEAK TO A SOLICITOR at this time:
Signature: John Randall
Time: 15:00   Date: 1/4/08
Reasons if given: IN A HURRY

Notification of named person: requested
Yes [ ] No [✓]
Nominated person: ....
Detainees signature: ....

12. FOREIGN NATIONALS
Embassy/Consulate informed: Yes [ ] No [ ]
Force Immigration Dept informed: Yes [ ] No [ ]

13. APPROPRIATE ADULT   **INTERPRETER**
Yes [ ] No [✓]   Yes [ ] No [✓]
Notices served, rights and grounds for detention explained in presence of Appropriate Adult/ Interpreter
Signature of A/Adult.......... Date.......... Time.......
Signature of Interpreter.......... Date.......... Time.......

NOTES: THE POLICE

'**Protect and serve**' are two key themes in the role of the police force, who see that by working together we can make communities safer places to be. To suggest, therefore, that all or even many arrests and 'bookings in' happen as portrayed in the last two exercises would be wrong. But as in any organisation there are occasions on which individuals and the organisations themselves make mistakes. In 1998 the Metropolitan Police Service was accused of being 'institutionally racist' by the inquiry led by Sir William Macpherson into the death of the black teenager Stephen Lawrence. However, in the years since, the police have worked hard to address some of these internal issues and are recognising increasingly the importance of working in partnership with all members of the community.

'**Safeguarding our community**': This is the strap line of Dyfed-Powys Police, and like other police forces it highlights the aim of the police to make our communities safer. This does not mean just safer for adults. Sir Ronnie Flannigan's report into policing in 2008 said neighbourhood policing builds 'stronger, more harmonious communities' and that 'neighbourhood policing staff often act as catalysts for building relationships between different groups, which increases mutual respect and civility' (Flannigan 2008: 6.44). It is fundamentally important that young people feel able to engage with neighbourhood policing, as this will not only offer them somewhere to turn if they witness or are a victim of crime, but also, as the result of better relationships, it will benefit the whole of the community, helping the police to do their job more effectively.

'**Listens and learns**': So say Greater Manchester Police in their vision statement. Like them, police throughout the country suggest a commitment to listen to what people say and to work to change things for the better. It is therefore important that young people work with the police as they look to build more positive relationships within communities. If young people feel that the police force is not providing them with the service that they deserve, then they need to say so. (See 'Helpful websites'.)

4.8 CONCLUSION

1. Review session

The law does not work how it might appear on TV or in films; there are steps or measures that the police must satisfy or take into account before they can use their powers. It is important that as citizens we recognise the powers the police have and their role in our community, so that we can work more effectively with them. But it is also important that we are aware of what our rights are.

Session outcomes should include participants:

o having a better understanding of what antisocial behaviour is

o having a greater awareness of police powers out on the streets

o developing further their ability to make an argument and to use listening skills

o furthering their knowledge of the law and their rights and responsibilities as citizens

o being empowered to participate more fully within society, through increased knowledge

o recognising what the police have to do and why, as part of working to make communities safer.

2. Check everyone is okay

If anyone does have any follow-up questions or is worried about anything, do give them an opportunity after the session to raise concerns with you. (See web addresses at the end of the session for more information.)

3. Date of next session

Project ideas

1. Do you think that antisocial behaviour is a problem? Explore with others of your own age what they think antisocial behaviour is and whether it is a real problem. What is its cause and how would you deal with it?

2. Put together a presentation raising awareness of young people's rights out on the streets for others. You could develop your own dramas (see Norton-Taylor 1999, below) about how a search should and should not be carried out, or create your own information flyers or posters.

3. Invite your local neighbourhood police officer to come and meet with your group, so that you can find out at first hand more about what the police do. This will also provide an opportunity to consider whether there are any barriers that need to be broken down, and how this could be done.

Helpful websites

- **www.adviceguide.org.uk** – online site of the Citizens Advice Bureau; includes pages on young people and the law, plus links to local legal advice centres. Provides separate guides to the law for Scotland, Northern Ireland, Wales and England. Has links to regional experts for further information in relation to aspects of law

- **www.blink.org.uk** – Black Information Link – more on human rights and race equality

- **www.childrenslegalcentre.com** – site of Children's Legal Centre; also offers freephone service for young people: 0800 7832187

- **www.homeoffice.gov.uk** – for information on PACE and other aspects of the criminal justice system

- **www.ipcc.gov.uk** – site of the Independent Police Complaints Commission

- **www.liberty-human-rights.org.uk** – Liberty, civil liberties organisation – more on young people's rights

- **www.opsi.gov.uk** – Office of Public Sector Information – to access Scottish legislation as well as that in the UK

- **www.scottishlaw.org.uk** – Scottish Law Online – some useful links to organisations involved in Criminal Justice work in Scotland

- **www.youngscot.org** – Young Scot – provides useful information for young people in Scotland on their rights, as well as offering a free helpline: 0808 8010338

BIBLIOGRAPHY

References

ACPO (2008) 'Stop and search statement.' Press release 30/1/08, ref 25/08.

BBC News (31/1/08) 'Is stop and search a good idea?' Accessed 27/3/08, http://news.bbc.co.uk/go/pr/fr/-/1/hi/uk/7218680.stm

Blink (2007) 'Keith Jarrett suggests an increase in police stop and search to curb spate of recent youth murders.' Press release 21/10/07.

Flannigan, R. (2008) *The Review of Policing*. London: Home Office.

Guardian, The (27/3/08) 'Balls to grant schools new search powers'

Holtam, J. (2001) *Criminal Litigation*. Bristol: Jordans.

Home Office (2007) *Crime in England and Wales 2006/07*. London: Home Office.

Ministry of Justice (2007a) *Arrests for Recorded Crime and the Operation of Certain Police Powers under PACE*. Statistical Bulletin. London: Ministry of Justice.

Ministry of Justice (2007b) *Statistics on Race and the Criminal Justice System 2006*. A Ministry of Justice publication under s95 of the Criminal Justice Act 1991. London: Ministry of Justice.

Norton-Taylor, R. (ed.) (1999) *The Colour of Justice*. London: Oberon Books.
This book is set out as a play based on transcripts of the Stephen Lawrence Inquiry.

Sunday Times, The (3/2/08) 'Stop and search saves lives'

Sunday Times, The (17/2/08) 'Police get electronic stop and search'

Sources of law

Criminal Procedures (Scotland) Act (1995). London: HMSO.

Police and Criminal Evidence Act (1984) (PACE). London: HMSO.

Stair Memorial Encyclopaedia (2008 – as updated). Edinburgh: Butterworths Law (Scotland).

Session 5

CITIZENSHIP IN PRACTICE

SESSION OVERVIEW

This session draws together some of the key themes from earlier in the course by following a case study that leads from a crime being committed to a police interview. This session follows a very practical format, relying on the group to use many of the skills that they have been developing throughout the course. It will review themes from each session, so do take the opportunity to spend time reviewing any issues that particularly stood out for your group.

There is a certain amount of preparation needed for this session, so do spend some time looking at the exercises, particularly the 'interview', so that you are clear about how you will do it. If there are two of you facilitating the sessions, then you will need to consider how you intend to divide the tasks. You may find it useful to split the participants into four groups right from the start; they will stay in these groups throughout this session.

Aims

- to review themes from earlier sessions
- specifically to re-consider the importance of mutual respect
- to put into practice the skills learnt throughout the course
- to consider what happens in a police interview.

Outcomes

Session outcomes will include participants:

- working together as a team
- having a strong understanding of the importance of giving and receiving respect
- gaining knowledge of what happens in a police interview
- consolidating themes from other sessions.

Session 5 timed outline

ACTION	TIME IN MINUTES	DESCRIPTION	RESOURCES	NOTES
1. Introduction	5	• welcome • refresh ground rules • re-cap Session 4 • introduce Session 5	Flipchart	
2. Course re-cap	10	Quiz, Sheet 5.2a, looking at themes from the earlier sessions. Answers provided on Sheet 5.2b. Use the questions to reconsider any specific themes discussed in earlier sessions.	5.2a 5.2b	
3. 'A crime is committed'	10	In pairs or small groups, use listening skills to find out what has happened. One group to act as 'victim' (Sheet 5.3a), the other as 'friend' (Sheet 5.3b).	5.3a 5.3b	
4. Search and find	10	In groups: read participants the scenarios and ask them to answer, using letters A and B. Go through answers, reminding group of stop and search and arrest powers.	5.4a 5.3b	
5. Break	5	If required, ask participants to start filling out the evaluation forms.	5.9	
6. Arriving at the police station	10	Remain in groups. Make sure participants are aware of the lawyer's interview with Jay. Ask participants to prepare an effective argument stating what concerns they have and what they want done. A member of the group to present the argument to the custody sergeant. (Arguments to last no more than 30 seconds.) Consider what makes an effective argument.	5.6	

Session 5 timed outline *continued*

7. Advising your client	10	Take groups through what the police and Jay say about the case. Explain the different options available for a police interview: ● answer questions ● no comment ● written statement. Ask groups to consider what advice they would give. Best advice: to answer questions.	5.7
8. Police interview	25	1. Divide group evenly: 'lawyers' and 'suspects'. 2. Go through information separately with these groups (Sheets 5.8a and b). 3. Groups to decide who will play the parts. 4. Interview 1 (Sheets 5.8c and d). 5. Discuss (Sheet 5.8c). 6. Interview 2 (Sheets 5.8c and e). 7. Discuss (Sheet 5.8c). 8. Conclusion. Respect given and received is the best way of people co-operating even in difficult situations. Without respect, the result is anger and resentment.	5.8a 5.8b 5.8c 5.8d 5.8e
9. Conclusion	5	1. Check all okay. 2. Re-cap course. 3. Thank you.	
Evaluation		See handout if required.	5.9

5.1 INTRODUCTION TO SESSION 5
Welcome

1. Welcome group to the session.

2. Ground rules.

3. Re-cap Session 4.

a) Remind the group that some of the issues you addressed in Session 4 included:

   ○ having a better understanding of what antisocial behaviour is

   ○ having a greater awareness of police powers out on the streets

   ○ developing further their ability to make an argument and to use listening skills

   ○ furthering their knowledge of the law and their rights and responsibilities as citizens

   ○ being empowered to participate more fully within society, through increased knowledge

   ○ recognising what the police have to do, and why, as part of working to make communities safer.

b) Ask if anyone has had any thoughts on the issues raised since the last session.

Introduce Session 5

Developing an awareness of mutual respect has been an important part of this course. In this session you will be reminded of how important respect is in breaking down barriers and in building effective relationships, as well as looking at some of the other themes from past sessions. In following a case study of a particular crime, you will have to use the knowledge and skills that you have picked up in previous sessions to successfully complete the tasks. The session breaks down into the following sections:

1. Introduction to Session 5

2. Course re-cap

3. 'A crime is committed'

4. Search and find

5. Break

6. Arriving at the police station

7. Advising your client

8. Police interview

9. Course conclusion.

5.2 COURSE RE-CAP

Exercise 5.2: Quiz

The purpose of this course has been to increase your knowledge and skills, so that you can be an active citizen, getting the most out of the communities that you live in.

Instructions: You can simply split the participants into groups and hand out quiz sheets (Sheet 5.2a), giving them a time limit (three minutes) to complete the questions, or you may wish to do the quiz in a different way, such as inviting two participants up to go head-to-head, representing the others. Add any other questions that revisit issues that were of particular interest to your group. Answers are on Sheet 5.2b.

Discuss: As you go through the answers, take the opportunity to refresh the group's memories of some of the key issues from earlier sessions.

QUIZ

Circle words or phrases, fill in the gaps and write your answers on the dotted lines.

Session 1

1. **Which stereotype is commonly used to describe young people when out in the neighbourhood?**

   helpful   yobs   snobs

2. **Name one danger of using stereotypes (bonus point if you can name more than one).**

   ....

3. **Which group is most at risk of murder?**

   teenagers   those aged 20–35 years   children under 1 year

4. **Mutual respect is important in breaking down barriers. Listening is a good way of showing respect. Name two barriers to good listening**

   ....

   ....

Session 2

5. **Bullying affects:**

   people in the army   people in schools   people when out in the neighbourhood

6. **Right and wrong is not fixed, it is flexible. What can help to shape the meaning that we give to our actions?**

    A D__ F __ __ __ __ __ __ N

7. **What question can we ask ourselves to help work out whether our action is acceptable or not?**

    . . . .

8. **Name two ways in which a crime might impact on a victim.**

    . . . .

    . . . .

Session 3

9. **Name one thing you can do to share a message effectively.**

    . . . .

10. **Who decides whether an action is a crime?**

    the police   Parliament   the community

11. **List two crimes in each section:**

Crimes against the person	Property crimes	Vehicle crimes	Antisocial behaviour

12. Name a group other than the police whose job it is to enforce the law.

....

13. Which of these actions could be seen as antisocial behaviour?

littering   hanging around   playing loud music
                                                         from a car

14. When searching, police must inform the detained person of:

GO__ __ __ __

15. You do not have to say anything but it may harm your defence if you do not mention when questioned something which you later rely on in court. Pick the right ending:

Do you under-   Anything you do   Anything you say
stand?   will be used against   can be given in
                       you.   evidence.

16. What is missing? At the police station you have the right to:

a) see a copy of the codes of practice

b) inform someone of your arrest

c) ....

QUIZ – ANSWERS

Session 1

1. **Which stereotype is commonly used to describe young people when out in the neighbourhood?**

helpful   (yobs)   snobs

2. **Name one danger of using stereotypes (bonus point if you can name more than one).**

lack accuracy, carry negative overtones, exaggerate difference, too broad

3. **Which group is most at risk of murder?**

teenagers   those aged 20–35 years   (children under 1 year)

4. **Mutual respect is important in breaking down barriers. Listening is a good way of showing respect. Name two barriers to good listening.**

Interrupting, asking multiple questions, moralising, blaming, ...

being indifferent, patronising . . . .

Session 2

5. **Bullying affects:**

(people in the army)   (people in schools)   (people when out in the neighbourhood)

6. **Right and wrong is not fixed, it is flexible. What can help to shape the meaning that we give to our actions?**

   A DEFINITION

7. **What question can we ask ourselves to help work out whether our action is acceptable or not?**

   Do our actions make us and those around us feel safe?
   ···

8. **Name two ways in which a crime might impact on a victim.**

   Shock, guilt, fear, anger (to name four)
   ···

Session 3

9. **Name one thing you can do to share a message effectively.**

   Stay calm, be respectful, listen
   ···

10. **Who decides whether an action is a crime?**

    the police    Parliament   the community

11. **List two crimes in each section:**

Crimes against the person	Property crimes	Vehicle crimes	Antisocial behaviour
• assault/battery • assault occasioning ABH • assault occasioning • GBH • obstructing a police officer • sexual offences (sexual assault, rape) • possession of drugs • intent to supply drugs • trafficking drugs • kidnap • murder	• theft • burglary • handling • fraud • criminal damage • obtaining property by deception • abstracting electricity • going equipped • arson	• taking a vehicle without consent • interfering with a vehicle • driving without proper documentation • driving while intoxicated through drink or drugs • making off without payment • failure to stop/report an accident • trespass/throwing stones on railways	• causing harassment, alarm or distress • affray • riot • offensive weapons • malicious communication • breach of antisocial behaviour orders • ticket touting

12. Name a group other than the police whose job it is to enforce the law.

. . . . Us, PCSOs, RSPCA Officers . . . .

13. Which of these actions could be seen as antisocial behaviour?

littering   hanging around   playing loud music from a car

14. When searching, police must inform the detained person of:

GO <u>W I S E</u>

15. You do not have to say anything but it may harm your defence if you do not mention when questioned something which you later rely on in court. Pick the right ending:

Do you under-
stand?

Anything you do
will be used against
you.

Anything you say
can be given in
evidence.

16. What is missing? At the police station you have the right to:

a) see a copy of the codes of practice

b) inform someone of your arrest

c) ...get legal advice . . . .

5.3 'A CRIME IS COMMITTED'

Group exercise 5.3: Using listening skills

Instructions

1. Split into groups of no more than four, or simply into pairs, one person to be the 'victim', one the 'friend', and any others to act as observers. The aim of the exercise is for the friend to get as much information out of the victim as possible by using good open questions and positive body language. You may wish to remind the group of these.

2. Give participants relevant handouts, one for the 'victim' (Sheet 5.3a), the other for the 'friend' (Sheet 5.3b). Give them time to read through.

DO EXERCISE.

Discuss: Briefly review the exercise, attending to how well the friend did. What kind of questions and actions encouraged the victims to talk; which did not?

'A CRIME IS COMMITTED'

Victims

You have been the victim of burglary. Yesterday, while you were out during the day, your house was broken into. Amongst the items that were stolen there was a new stereo system you had just bought. You had got a weekend job to pay for it. You obviously feel cross and angry that the stereo system has been taken.

You may also have other feelings about the crime. Think quickly what these might be. For example, how do you feel about someone breaking into your house and walking around the space that you live in?

All your friend has been told is that you have been a victim of a crime – he/she knows nothing else.

- Only open up to them if they ask you good open questions. Listen out for who? what? when? where? how?

- Are they showing good listening skills? If not, don't answer their questions.

If you don't have information in relation to some of the questions they ask you, make it up to keep the role-play going.

'A CRIME IS COMMITTED'

Friends

You have heard that one of your good friends has been a victim of crime. You want to find out how they are and what has happened to them.

Spend a few moments thinking about:

- good open questions (who? what? when? where? how?)

- good open and attentive body language

- what your opening question is going to be.

5.4 SEARCH AND FIND

Group exercise 5.4: Police powers

Instructions:

1. The following exercise is a speed quiz, with points going to the group that answers quickest and with the correct answer. Split participants into small groups A and B. (Use Sheets 5.4a and 5.4b.) Keep scores on the flipchart or whiteboard.

2. Read out this scenario and answer the questions that follow:

> The police are searching for a stereo system stolen recently from a house in Langley. The Police Community Support Officers have also been asked to keep their eyes open.

1. A PCSO, while walking round the park, notices two young people. One hands an item to the other that looks like a knife. Can the PCSO search them?

   a) Yes   b) No

   No. The PCSO has no power of search in this situation, unless in a designated area and with a police constable.

2. A police officer on the other side of the park also notices something happening. Can she search the young people for the stereo system?

   a) Yes   b) No

   No. There is no way that the young people could be hiding a stereo system on them, therefore there can be no reasonable suspicion that this particular item will be found.

3. A car is stopped early in the morning. In the car, as well as the driver, the officers see some tools, gloves and a balaclava. When asked what this was for, the driver says, 'I am a builder.' Can the police search the car?

   a) Yes   b) No

   Yes. The time of day, the items in the car and the man's response could all add up to reasonable suspicion that this individual may have other 'prohibited items' in the vehicle.

4. The following day Jay is driving a red Ford Escort. The rear brake light is broken. Can the police stop the car?

   a) Yes   b) No

   Yes. A police officer in uniform has the power to stop any vehicle on the road; they do not need reasonable suspicion. (This is a different power from PACE.)

5. The car belongs to Lee, Jay's sister's boyfriend. He has only just bought it. Jay has permission to drive the car and has insurance and has passed his test. Jay has never been in trouble before, although he knows Lee has. An intelligence flag is shown on the vehicle when the officers radio in the registration number. It may have been connected to a burglary a number of years ago. Can the police search the car?

a) Yes   b) No

Yes. The intelligence flag is enough to create reasonable suspicion that this vehicle may contain 'prohibited items'.

6. The police start to search the car. In the glove compartment they find a whole lot of rubbish, bits of magazines, cartons from McDonald's, a couple of tapes and a Stanley knife. They walk round to the back of the car where they open the boot. Inside is a black stereo system, without any leads, matching the description of the item stolen. Can the police arrest Jay?

a) Yes   b) No

Yes. He has been found in possession of a stereo system matching the one stolen. Even though there may be an explanation for this, the police can arrest him on 'suspicion' of being involved. NOTE: An offensive weapon has also been found in the car, for which he can also be arrested.

7. Can the police then search Jay?

a) Yes   b) No

Yes. They can search anyone after arrest, using different powers from PACE, for anything that might cause Jay or the officers harm, or that could be used in an escape or for anything related to an offence.

8. In Jay's coat pocket there is a very small amount of cannabis. The police arrest Jay again. They go to handcuff Jay's hands. Can the police use handcuffs?

a) Yes   b) No

Yes. The police can use handcuffs to protect themselves and the detained person. However, they can only use force that is reasonable.

5.5 BREAK

5.6 ARRIVING AT THE POLICE STATION

Group exercise 5.6: Jay's story continues

Instructions

1. Stay in the same groups.

2. Read out the information in the box below, or, if you prefer, give out Sheet 5.6 to the participants.

3. Ask groups to imagine they are Jay's lawyer. They are to put together an argument of no longer than 30 seconds, stating to the custody sergeant (you) *what concerns they have over Jay's treatment* and *what they want done about it.*

Jay arrives at the police station and is booked in. Jay chooses to have a lawyer. Your group is now the lawyer. You arrive at the police station.

On arriving, you check the custody record. Amongst other things you note that your client has said that he doesn't want to see a doctor. After talking to the arresting officers, you then go to speak to your client.

You go to shake Jay's hand and notice immediately that Jay's wrist is swollen. Jay tells you: 'They put the handcuffs on so tight, my wrists hurt a lot now. Look at how swollen this one is, I can't even move it. I asked to see the doctor but they ignored me, so I asked to see a copy of the codes of practice and they told me you had to be over 20 to be allowed to see it.'

Question: What concerns do you have? And what would you want done about it? Prepare a clear, respectful and effective argument to present to the custody sergeant.

DO EXERCISE.

Discuss: Look for quality and effectiveness of arguments, as well as content, which should include:

- Your client does want to see a doctor, contrary to what is in the custody record. Access to the doctor needs to be arranged as soon as possible.

- Your client does have the right to see a copy of the codes of practice (you do not need to be over 20) and this should be dealt with immediately.

- Your client appears to have a bad injury as a result of the way the handcuffs were applied. This should be raised and questions asked about whether the force used was reasonable.

- You may feel it is appropriate to demand to speak to a more senior officer.

ARRIVING AT THE POLICE STATION

Jay's story continues

You are Jay Thompson's lawyer.

Using the following information, present a respectful and effective argument to the custody sergeant of no more than 30 seconds, stating:

- what concerns you

- what you want done about it.

Prepare as a group and then choose one of you to present the argument.

Jay arrives at the police station and is booked in. Jay chooses to have a lawyer. Your group is now the lawyer. You arrive at the police station.

On arriving, you check the custody record. Amongst other things you note that your client has said that he doesn't want to see a doctor. After talking to the arresting officers, you then go to speak to your client.

You go to shake Jay's hand and notice immediately that Jay's wrist is swollen. Jay tells you: 'They put the handcuffs on so tight, my wrists hurt a lot now. Look at how swollen this one is, I can't even move it. I asked to see the doctor but they ignored me, so I asked to see a copy of the codes of practice and they told me you had to be over 20 to be allowed to see it.'

5.7 ADVISING YOUR CLIENT

Group exercise 5.7: The lawyer's role

The idea of the exercise is simply to raise awareness of the role of the lawyer, as well as to provide participants with information they will need for the next exercise. Decisions on how to advise a client are complicated and take a lot of training, so do not spend too much time on it.

Instructions

1. Participants stay in their groups – they are still Jay's lawyer.

2. Read through together the information on Sheet 5.7, 'Advising your client'. There is a lot of information on this sheet, which will be used in the next exercise as well.

3. As well as reading the general information, look together at the three different options for advice at the bottom of the page.

4. Invite the groups to think how they would advise Jay.

DO EXERCISE.

Answer (to discuss): The best advice would be to answer questions. Jay appears to have a good defence to the charge of burglary, offensive weapon and assault. Rather than trying to deny possession of the cannabis, admit the offence; he may just receive a caution (as he hasn't offended before).

ADVISING YOUR CLIENT

The lawyer's role

As a lawyer your main job at the police station is to advise your client about what they should do in the police interview. To do this effectively you need to have spoken to your client, sharing with them the police account and then listening to what your client has to say.

The police said:

At 2235hrs. on 1 March PC Mitchell and PC Lloyd were on duty in a marked police car. They saw a red Ford Escort registration E241 JJR. The car was stopped. The officers searched the car and found a black Stanley knife in the glove compartment. Jay Thompson, who was the driver of the car, was then arrested and cautioned. The time was 2238hrs.

The officers continued to search the car and found a black stereo system in the boot. There were no leads with it and it matched the description of an item recently stolen from the area.

On searching Jay Thompson a small quantity of a herbal-like substance was found in the right coat pocket. As PC Lloyd took the cannabis out of JT's pocket, JT said, 'Come off it, it's only a bit of puff.' JT was then arrested and cautioned. JT was then handcuffed. During this JT became agitated and attempted to headbutt PC Lloyd.

JT has been arrested on suspicion of being in possession of an offensive weapon, being in possession of a controlled drug, burglary, and assault on a police officer. The police want to obtain further evidence through a police interview.

You explain to Jay that, before giving advice on what to do in the interview, you must first hear what he has to say.

Jay tells you:

I was just borrowing Lee's car, he's my sister's boyfriend. I have all the proper paperwork and stuff. I had just been to drop my mum off at the station and was driving home, it was the first time I had used the car for weeks. I had no idea there was a knife in the glove compartment. It is certainly not mine. And as for the stereo system – I had never seen that before either, as I said I had only just borrowed the car to take my mum to the station. But I must admit the cannabis was mine, but it is only cannabis and is only a small amount for my own use. And what, they are accusing me of assaulting them, look at my wrists, they're red as anything, this one is swelling up, I can't even move it. When the handcuffs went on I just reacted to the pain, my head went up, and I must of knocked one of the officers, it was an accident. I would never do something like that on purpose.

Question: Choosing from the options below, what advice should be given to Jay on what to do in the interview?

1. **Answer questions**: If there is a clear and solid defence. This might also be advised if the client wanted to admit the offence, leading to a caution (or a reprimand or warning for young offenders), or if it was felt important that mitigation (an explanation for the offence) needed to be put on the record.

2. **No comment**: This would be advised if there are concerns about the client's welfare or there is a chance of the client incriminating himself. Also, no comment may be advised if there is no defence or there is a lack of information on which to base a defence.

3. **Written statement**: This allows a suspect to put forward a partial defence, but without the risk of incriminating themselves by answering questions in relation to evidence not yet received, or where the defence is not so strong.

5.8 POLICE INTERVIEW

Group exercise 5.8: The police interview Jay

The following exercise will simulate a police interview. However, in so doing it will raise a broader point about the centrality of respect, both in enforcing the law, and within society more generally. There is guidance for two interviews (see facilitator's notes on Sheet 5.8c), one done properly, the other not. For each actual interview you will want only one participant as Jay, and one other as the lawyer. The facilitator will play the police officer (or two officers, if there are two facilitators). Facilitators need to read in advance the notes on Sheet 5.8c.

Instructions

1. Participants stay in groups. Choose half the groups to look at the exercise from the point of view of the lawyer, the other half from the point of view of the suspect.

2. Give out the relevant handouts: Sheet 5.8a for the 'suspects', Sheet 5.8b for the 'lawyers'. The groups will also need to keep the information on the lawyer's role (Sheet 5.7) from the last exercise. If there are two facilitators one could go through the handout for the 'suspects', while the other does the same for the 'lawyers'.

3. Give the groups time to go through their handouts and decide which individual will take on the roles.

4. *Interview 1*

   Ask those not directly taking part to watch carefully. Facilitators use the script on Sheet 5.8d.

5. *Discuss Interview 1*

   After each interview, ask those involved how they felt. Did they feel they could get their point across; did they feel fairly treated?

   Interview 1 can make people in the 'suspect' role feel quite uncomfortable, even angry, as they are not able to get their point of view across.

   The 'lawyer' should have been involved throughout, challenging: the positioning of the chair, the aggressive attitude of the officer, questions about other offences, the officer's standing up, multiple questions, irrelevant questions, and more. Was the lawyer able to bring some kind of order to the interview? Was he/she able to protect the suspect effectively?

6. *Interview 2*

7. *Discuss Interview 2*

This is a very different experience. The nature of the questions and the more respectful approach immediately encourage the suspect to open up, and it is much easier for the story to be shared. Working in this way, the police officer gets the information that is needed and the suspect feels that he has been fairly treated.

8. Exercise conclusion.

This exercise shows the vast difference it makes if you treat someone with respect. The result is that barriers are broken down, even in difficult situations. When people are respected they feel as though their voice is heard, that they are treated fairly, with the result that they want to co-operate. Being disrespectful only leads to anger and resentment and a strong desire not to communicate. This message applies not only in police stations (which is why the police are trained to follow the model in Interview 2), but absolutely everywhere we come into contact with other people.

THE POLICE INTERVIEW JAY

Notes for 'suspects'

In this interview you are to play the part of Jay Thompson. You are 18 years old and you want to get all this dealt with as quickly as possible. You are perfectly happy to co-operate with the police if it will get you out of the police station more quickly, but you are not prepared to admit to anything that you did not do.

You have asked for a lawyer. Your lawyer has suggested that you answer questions in the interview as you have a good defence to the charges on which you have been arrested. The lawyer advises you to admit to being in possession of the cannabis.

As a group: Go through Sheet 5.7, 'Advising your client'. Remind yourself what happened earlier and think about some of the questions that you might get asked in the interview.

Choose one person to play Jay in the interview.

In the interview, try to answer the questions as best you can. If you don't know the answer, say so.

THE POLICE INTERVIEW JAY

Notes for 'lawyers'

You are a lawyer acting for 18-year-old Jay Thompson at Langley Police Station. Your role is to protect your client's legal rights.

You have already spoken to the police and your client about the alleged offence. You have advised your client to answer questions in the police interview, as you believe he has a strong defence to the charges of being in possession of an offensive weapon, burglary and assaulting a police officer. You also believe that your client should admit to being in possession to a small amount of cannabis for personal use.

As a group: Review the information that you have been given about the case so far, using particularly Sheet 5.7, 'Advising your client'. Think of some of the questions your client might get asked in the interview and how you many need to protect him. The following list may help you – look at it carefully.

Police are not allowed to do the following in interview:

- ask multiple questions

- shout

- place the lawyer in a position from which he/she can't advise their client

- ask about offences for which the suspect has not been arrested

- ask about irrelevant issues

- stand up

- interrupt

- pressurise

- lead the client into answering questions

- use abusive language.

If for any reason the officer does one of these, it is your responsibility to stop it and to make sure Jay is being asked reasonable questions relevant to the investigation of the offences for which he was arrested.

Choose one of you to play the part of the lawyer during the interview.

THE POLICE INTERVIEW JAY

Notes for facilitators – Interviews 1 and 2

INTERVIEW 1

You are to play the part of PC Lloyd. This interview will show you how things should *not* be done. It will mean you taking on an aggressive, disrespectful attitude, believing that Jay is lying and that Jay is guilty of all the offences that he has been arrested for. Give Jay time to answer questions or desist from improper actions only if the lawyer insists on it.

The lawyers have been provided with the following information.

Police are not allowed to do the following in interview:

- ask multiple questions

- shout

- place the lawyer in a position from which he/she can't advise their client

- ask about offences for which the suspect has not been arrested

- ask about irrelevant issues

- stand up

- interrupt

- pressurise

- lead the client into answering questions

- use abusive language.

Sheet 5.8d will lead you through the interview. Do feel free to develop some of the dialogue yourself, using the information provided as a guide through the interview.

Prior to the interview, send the lawyer and suspect out of the room. Find a table and position it with two chairs facing each other, one for the suspect, the other for the police officer, and a third chair directly behind the suspect's for the lawyer. It is also effective if you can find a tape recorder and blank tape, so that you can record the interview. Get other participants to move their chairs round so they can see.

Refresh your memory of the incident, using Sheet 5.7, 'Advising your client'.

Sheet 5.8c cont.

When you are ready to start, invite the suspect and lawyer to come in, and show them their seats. Create a fuss if the lawyer wants to move his/her chair, but do allow it.

Tapes are sealed before use. If you have a new cassette tape, use that, otherwise you could pretend by wrapping old tape in cling film before the session. Put the tape into the tape player and press 'Record'.

Now see Sheet 5.8d, 'Notes for facilitators – Interview 1: Script'.

INTERVIEW 2

In this interview you are still PC Lloyd – however, take on a far more professional and respectful attitude towards Jay. You are interested in investigating this offence properly and ensuring that those that you work with are treated fairly and given a proper opportunity to provide their side of the story.

Send the new 'Jay' and 'lawyer' out. Use the desk again, this time putting the lawyer's chair next to the suspect's. Follow the same procedure as before with the tapes.

Use the script provided on Sheet 5.8e, 'Notes for facilitators – Interview 2: Script', and give the suspect plenty of time to answer the questions. The lawyer should not need to get involved at all.

THE POLICE INTERVIEW JAY

Notes for facilitators – Interview 1: Script

[Say the following: (fill in blanks)]

The date is…

The time is…

This interview is being tape recorded at…[*name of police station*]. At the end of the interview, Jay, I will give you a notice explaining what will happen to the tapes. I am PC Lloyd, collar number 2934. There are no other officers present.

What is your full name? [*Ask Jay.*]

Also present is… [*Ask lawyer.*]

Let me just remind you of the caution. It is this: 'You do not have to say anything, but it may harm your defence if you do not mention when questioned something which you later rely on in court. Anything you do say can be given in evidence.'

Late last night you were arrested for a string of different offences and I am now going to question you about them.

Did you nick the CD player?

I don't believe you. Did you nick the CD player?

[*Raise your voice as you speak the following.*] Didn't you mean to say yes? Yes, I did nick it. Yes, I did burgle that house. Yes, I did do it – do you agree?

Do you agree burglary is a horrible crime?

So why do it?

Did you take that knife into the house with you so you could stab someone if they tried to stop you taking their stuff?

[*Stand up.*] If all you are going to do is lie all day, then I might as well get you charged right now. Just tell me the truth.

How many people have you stabbed or threatened to stab with that knife?

Are you telling me you are not aggressive? You tried to knock me out, you assaulted me, didn't you, standing up and headbutting me on purpose. Do you hit anyone who gets in your way? Headbutting is a bit cowardly, isn't it?

Tell me about the drugs.

Are they good for you?

Is it against the law to have them on you?

Yes, it is, and you had drugs on you, didn't you?

I've heard enough – that's the end of the interview.

Do you want to add anything?... [*Interrupt if Jay answers.*] I doubt it, it would only be a lie.

Ending this interview at... [*time*].

THE POLICE INTERVIEW JAY

Notes for facilitators – Interview 2: Script

The date is…

The time is…

This interview is being tape recorded at…[*name of police station*]. At the end of the interview, Jay, I will give you a notice explaining what will happen to the tapes. I am PC Lloyd, collar number 2934. There are no other officers present.

What is your full name? [*Ask Jay.*]

Also present is… [*Ask lawyer.*]

Let me just remind you of the caution. It is this: 'You do not have to say anything, but it may harm your defence if you do not mention when questioned something which you later rely on in court. Anything you do say can be given in evidence.' Do you understand the caution?

You were stopped in a car last night. When the car was searched a Stanley knife was found, for which you were arrested. A stereo system, which matched the description of an item stolen, was also found in the boot of the car. You were arrested on suspicion of burglary. Following the arrest you were searched and a herbal-like substance was found in your pocket. You were again arrested for being in possession of controlled drugs. When you were handcuffed you reacted, headbutting my colleague, and again we arrested you for a further offence of assaulting a police officer. I would now like to hear your side of the story and will give you an opportunity to tell me about each of these suspected offences individually. Do you understand?

Tell me what happened last night.

Who owns the car?

Why was there a Stanley knife in the car?

What do you know about the stereo system found in the boot?

What was the herbal substance in your pocket?

Why did you headbutt my colleague?

[*Repeat what has been presented to you during the interview and ask Jay whether you have understood it all right.*]

Is there anything you would like to add or clarify following this interview?

I am concluding this interview at…[*time*].

5.9 COURSE CONCLUSION

1. **Check everyone is okay**

2. **Course overview – aims and objectives**

    Young people out in the neighbourhood are often a target for adults who see them as a nuisance and as a threat, with the result that young people are not treated with the respect they deserve. This course has been designed to help YOU change this. It has asked you to think about how you want to be seen by others, what behaviour is right and what is wrong, why the law covers certain behaviour, and what the law says and can do. You should be able to recognise that you have certain rights, but these rights are only really effective when you recognise your responsibilities as well. You should now be better equipped to know your rights and responsibilities within your community – and take on your role as an active citizen.

    Question: Does the group feel they know more now than they did at the beginning of the course? What has been most useful?

3. **Thank participants for taking part**

4. **Complete evaluation if required**

Evaluation

You may wish to evaluate the sessions to give you ideas for using the material in the future. We would also be very interested to hear how you get on with the course, and any thoughts or ideas that facilitators and participants have. See the contact details on the Act 4 website, listed below.

Please make use of the evaluation form (Sheet 5.9), or adapt to suit, either in its given form, or by adapting it to suit any comments you wish to add.

About Act 4

Act 4 is a charity that looks to equip children so that they can make a positive difference within the world around them. Based on Christian values, the charity develops educational programmes and community events that aim to support children and young people to make the most of their potential.

For additional support, resources and ideas on getting involved please see: www.act4.org.uk

We would be very keen to hear any thoughts or feedback you may have on the material presented in this book. See the contact details on the website.

EVALUATION FORM

1. **What was the most useful thing that you learnt?**

    ....

    ....

    ....

2. **What did you enjoy most?**

    ....

    ....

    ....

3. **What did you not enjoy?**

    ....

    ....

    ....

4. **What would you change about the course?**

    ....

    ....

    ....

5. **Any other comments?**

    ....

    ....

    ....

Thank you!